SAINT AUGUSTINE

ON THE TWO CITIES

Selections from
THE CITY OF GOD

Edited by

F. W. STROTHMANN
Stanford University

FREDERICK UNGAR PUBLISHING CO.
NEW YORK

MILESTONES
OF THOUGHT
in the History of Ideas

General Editor
F. W. STROTHMANN
Stanford University

Thirteenth Printing, 1980

ISBN 0-8044-6791-9

Library of Congress Catalog Card Number: 57–13344

Printed in the United States of America

INTRODUCTION

AURELIUS AUGUSTINUS was born in 354 A.D. in Tagaste in North Africa. His mother, St. Monica, was a Christian. During his youth he studied rhetoric and became interested in philosophy. As a teacher of rhetoric he went to Milan where he was converted to Christianity in 387. From 396 to the time of his death in 430, he was Bishop of Hippo Regius in North Africa.

Combining in himself both the mature classical tradition of Rome and the vitality of a newly found faith, he became one of the most influential teachers of Western Christianity. Of his numerous works, the *Confessions* and the *City of God* are the most widely known.

The immediate occasion of writing the *City of God* was the sack of Rome by the Goths in 410 A.D. The fall of Rome —for centuries *Roma aeterna,* the unchallenged mistress of the Mediterranean world, symbol and center of Western civilization—was a profound shock for all who lived in her protective shadow. Was this catastrophe, culminating a long period of gradual decline, the result of the fact that too many Romans, turning away from the gods that had led them to victory and domination, had accepted Christianity? Augustine set out to answer this question in the *City of God.*

But under the pen of its author—it took Augustine thirteen years to write the *City of God*—the work became more than a defense against unjust accusations: it became a major work on the Christian philosophy of history and a treatise on the relation between Church and State.

As a philosophy of history—"history" in the sense of "history of Man"—it has deeply influenced and still influences our thinking. For Augustine, history, in a way, "runs on rails": a straight predetermined line, foreknown by God, runs from the beginning, when Adam was created, inexorably toward the end, when all human history will cease with the manifestation of the City of God.

To be sure, in modern secularized variations of this concept, both the Augustinian beginning and the Augustinian end have been "cut off": the beginning is hidden in the impenetrable past of the race, and the end is hidden from our eyes in the unimaginable glory of unending progress. But whether the road into the future loses itself, to use Bellamy's optimistic phrase, "in light"—a concept that has been a vital influence since the eighteenth century—or whether it loses itself, since Marx, in the glorious mire of a classless bureaucracy, the "straight-line-philosophy" still dominates our historical thinking and planning, in spite of Toynbee and Spengler.

The important difference between Augustine and the moderns is the fact that the end, i.e., the establishment of a city or community which will last forever, will come for the modern non-Augustinian as the direct natural result of enlightened human endeavor, whereas for Augustine the end will come as the result of divine action employed in opposition to human endeavor. The eternal city, Augustine fervently believes, will be established. It will be established, however, not by human beings but by God, who will terminate man's rebellious attempt to build the City of Man upon the contrary-to-fact assumption that man's longing can be stilled by man rather than by God.

The problem of the relation between Church and State, the problem, that is, of how much to give to Caesar and how much to God, is as old as Christianity. Totally unlike certain later Christian totalitarians, Augustine does *not* propose to force upon the children of the earthly city a pattern of life natural only for the citizens of the heavenly city. Neither does he condemn the latter to a life of civic inactivity. The city of God must support the ordered peace of the earthly city. For in the first place, it cannot physically separate itself from the earthly city; and in the second place, this peace, considered in itself, is a legitimate good and thereby an obligatory goal for every Christian. As long as the earthly city makes no atttempt to force the heavenly city to abandon the one supreme Creator Good for the sake of created goods, the two cities have a common task: to secure those lesser goods without which human existence would become impossible. But peaceful coexistence gives way to persecution when the earthly city, demanding more than legitimate cooperation, insists that the city of God, like itself, commit idolatry by absolutizing values which are, in fact, not absolute. The last concentrated effort by the earthly city during the reign of Antichrist to force the heavenly city into idolatry will be frustrated when God calls an end to history.

Augustine's basic philosophy of history is still shared by millions of our contemporaries. Current books such as Josef Pieper's remarkable treatise toward a philosophy of history, *The End of Time,* testify to the continuing influence of the *City of God.*

SELECTED BIBLIOGRAPHY

S. Aurelii Augustini. *De Civitate Dei Contra Paganos*. Edited by J. E. C. Welldon, D.D., 2 volumes. London: Society for Promoting Christian Knowledge, and New York: The Macmillan Co., 1924.

The Works of Aurelius Augustine. A new translation. Edited by the Rev. Marcus Dods, M.A. Vols. I and II, *The City of God*. Translated by the Rev. Marcus Dods, M.A. Edinburgh: T. and T. Clark, 1871–1872.

Basic Writings of Saint Augustine. Edited by Whitney J. Oates. New York: Random House, 1948.

A Monument to St. Augustine. New York: Lincoln Mac-Veagh, the Dial Press, 1930.

Mommsen, Theodor E. *St. Augustine and the Christian Idea of Progress. Journal of the History of Ideas,* Vol. XII, pp. 346–374.

NOTE

The text presented follows, with only a few changes, the translation of the *De Civitate Dei* by Marcus Dods. Since the 1100 pages of the complete text form an almost forbidding barrier to the modern student, an attempt has been made to select, in a way which does not destroy the major argument, only those passages—and there are many of them —which still command interest and attention. Numbers in parentheses indicate the chapter of the book from which each passage has been taken. For the sake of better reading, deletions within each chapter are not indicated, but can easily be located by comparing the selections presented with the complete text.

BOOK I

The fall of Rome was a consequence of degeneration, not of the ascent of Christianity and the abandonment of heathen gods.

Instead of thanking Christ for still being alive, many pagans who survived the sack of Rome now blame Christ and the Christians for what is actually an inevitable consequence of their own degeneration.

The glorious city of God is my theme in this work, which you, my dearest son Marcellinus, suggested, and which is due you by my promise. I have undertaken its defense against those who prefer their own gods to the Founder of this city, a city surpassingly glorious, whether we view it as it still lives by faith in this fleeting course of time and sojourns as a pilgrim in the midst of the ungodly, or whether we view it as it shall dwell in the fixed stability of its eternal seat, which it now expects in patience, waiting until "righteousness be turned into judgment" † and it obtain, by virtue of its excellence, final victory and perfect peace.

A great work this, and an arduous; but God is my helper. For I am aware what ability is requisite to persuade the proud how great is the virtue of humility, which raises us by divine grace above all earthly dignities that totter on this shifting scene. For the King and Founder of this city of which we speak has in Scripture uttered to His people a dictum of the divine law in these words: "God resisteth the proud, but giveth grace unto the humble." (Jas. 4, 6 and I Peter 5,5)

As the plan of the work we have undertaken requires and as occasion offers, we must speak also of the earthly city, which, though it be mistress of the nations, is itself ruled by

† Ps. 94, 15 rendered otherwise from English version.

1

its lust of rule. For to this earthly city belong the enemies against whom I have to defend the city of God. Many of them, indeed, being reclaimed from their ungodly error, have become sufficiently creditable citizens of the heavenly city; but many are so inflamed with hatred against it and so ungrateful to its Redeemer for His signal benefits as to forget that they would now be unable to utter a single word against it, had they not found in its sacred places, as they fled from the enemy's steel, that life in which they now boast themselves.

Have not those very Romans who were spared by the barbarians for Christ's sake become enemies to the name of Christ? The reliquaries of the martyrs and the churches of the apostles bear witness to this; for in the sack of Rome they were open sanctuary for all who fled to them, whether they were Christian or Pagan. Thus escaped multitudes who now reproach the Christian religion and impute to Christ the ills that have befallen their city; but the preservation of their own life—a boon which they owe to the respect entertained for Christ by the barbarians—they attribute not to our Christ, but to their own good luck. They ought rather, had they any right perceptions, to attribute the severities and hardships inflicted by their enemies to that divine providence which is wont to reform the depraved manners of men by chastisement and which exercises with similar afflictions the righteous and praiseworthy—either transporting them, when they have passed through the trial, to a better world, or detaining them still on earth for other purposes. And they ought to attribute it to the spirit of these Christian times that, contrary to the custom of war, these bloodthirsty barbarians spared them, and spared them for Christ's sake, whether this mercy was actually shown just anywhere or in those places specially dedicated to Christ's name, of which the very largest were selected as sanctuaries, that full scope might thus be given to the expansive compassion which desired that a large multitude might find shelter there. Therefore ought they to give God thanks and with sincere confession flee for refuge to His name, so that they may escape the punishment of eternal fire —they who with lying lips took upon them this name that they might escape the punishment of present destruction. For of those whom you see insolently and shamelessly insulting the servants of Christ, there are numbers who would not have escaped that destruction and slaughter had they not pretended that they themselves were Christ's servants. Yet now, in ungrateful pride and most impious madness and at the risk of being punished in everlasting darkness, they perversely oppose the name under which they fraudulently protected themselves for the sake of enjoying the light of this brief life. (1)

All the spoiling, then, which Rome was exposed to in the recent calamity, all the slaughter, plundering, burning, and misery, was the result of the custom of war. But what was novel was that savage barbarians showed themselves in so gentle a guise that the largest churches were chosen and set apart for the purpose of being filled with the people to whom quarter was given, and that in them none were slain, from them none forcibly dragged; that into them many were led by their relenting enemies to be set at liberty, and that from them none were led into slavery by merciless foes. Whoever does not see that this is to be attributed to the name of Christ and to the Christian temper is blind; whoever sees this and gives no praise is ungrateful; whoever hinders any one from praising it is mad. (7)

Will some one say, why, then, was this divine compassion extended even to the ungodly and ungrateful? Why, but because it was the mercy of Him who daily "maketh His sun to rise on the evil and on the good, and sendeth rain on the just and on the unjust." (Matt. 5, 45) (8)

But, it is added, many Christians were slaughtered and put to death in a hideous variety of cruel ways. Well, that death is not to be judged an evil which is the end of a good life; for death becomes evil only by the retribution which follows it. They, then, who are destined to die, need not be careful to inquire what death they are to die, but into what place death will usher them. And since Christians are well aware that the death of the godly pauper whose sores the dogs licked was far bettter than that of the wicked rich man who lay in purple and fine linen, what harm could these terrific deaths do to the dead who had lived well? (11)

The whole family of God has a consolation of its own, a consolation which cannot deceive and which has in it a surer hope than the tottering and falling affairs of earth can afford. They will not refuse the discipline of this temporal life, in which they are schooled for life eternal, nor will they lament their experience of it; for the good things of earth they use as pilgrims who are not detained by them, and its ills either prove or improve them. As for those who express contempt for their uprightness and, when ills befall them, say, "Where is thy God?" (Ps. 43, 3) we may ask them where their own gods are when they suffer the very calamities for the sake of avoiding which they worship their gods or maintain they ought to be worshipped. (29)

Why in your calamities do you complain of Christianity, unless because you desire to enjoy your luxurious license unrestrained and to lead an abandoned and profligate life without the interruption of any uneasiness or disaster? For certainly your desire for peace, and prosperity, and plenty is not prompted by any purpose of using these blessings honestly, that is to say, with moderation, sobriety, temperance, and piety; for your purpose rather is to run riot in an endless variety of sottish pleasures and thus to generate from your prosperity a moral pestilence which will prove a thousand-fold more disastrous than the fiercest enemies. It was such a calamity as this that Scipio,[1] your chief pontiff, your best man in the judgment of the whole senate, feared when he refused to agree to the destruction of Carthage, Rome's rival; and opposed Cato,[1] who advised its destruction. He feared security, that enemy of weak minds, and he perceived that a

[1] Publius Cornelius Scipio Nasica Corculum, Pontifex Maximus in 150 B.C., fought Cato (+149 B.C.) who demanded the destruction of Carthage,

wholesome fear would be a fit guardian for the citizens. And he was not mistaken: the event proved how wisely he had spoken. For when Carthage was destroyed and the Roman republic delivered from its great cause of anxiety, a crowd of disastrous evils forthwith resulted from the prosperous condition of things. First concord was weakened and destroyed by bloody seditions; then followed civil wars, which brought in their train such massacres, such bloodshed, such lawless and cruel proscription and plunder, that those Romans who, in the days of their virtue, had expected injury only at the hands of their enemies, now that their virtue was lost, suffered greater cruelties at the hands of their fellow-citizens. The lust of rule, which with other vices existed among the Romans in more unmitigated intensity than among any other people, after it had taken possession of the more powerful few, subdued under its yoke the rest, worn and wearied. (30)

For at what point would that lust of power cease and rest when once it has lodged in a proud spirit, until, by a succession of honors, it has reached regal power? And to obtain such honors nothing avails but unscrupulous ambition. But unscrupulous ambition has nothing to work upon, save in a nation corrupted by avarice and luxury. Moreover, a people becomes avaricious and luxurious by prosperity; and it was this which that very prudent man Nasica [2] was endeavouring to avoid when he opposed the destruction of the greatest, strongest, wealthiest city of Rome's enemy. He thought that thus fear would act as a curb on lust, and that lust, being curbed, would not run riot in luxury, and that, luxury being prevented, avarice would be at an end; and that these vices being banished, virtue would flourish and increase to the great profit of the state; and liberty, the fit companion of virtue, would abide unfettered. For similar reasons and animated by the same considerate patriotism, that same chief pontiff [2] of yours—I still refer to him who was adjudged Rome's best man without one dissentient voice—threw cold

[2] Cp. Note 1. It was in 155 B.C. that P. C. Scipio Nasica Corculum persuaded the Senate to stop the construction of a theatre.

water on the proposal of the senate to build a circle of seats round the theatre, and in a very weighty speech warned them against allowing the luxurious manners of Greece to sap the Roman manliness, and persuaded them not to yield to the enervating and emasculating influence of foreign licentiousness. (31)

Oh infatuated men, what is this blindness, or rather madness, which possesses you? How is it that while, as we hear, even the eastern nations are bewailing your ruin, and while powerful states in the most remote parts of the earth are mourning your fall as a public calamity, you yourselves should be crowding to the theatres, should be pouring into them and filling them, and, in short, be playing a madder part now than ever before? Depraved by good fortune and not chastened by adversity, what you desire in the restoration of a peaceful and secure state is not the tranquillity of the commonwealth, but the impunity of your own vicious luxury. Scipio wished you to be hard pressed by an enemy, that you might not abandon yourselves to luxurious manners; but so abandoned are you that not even when crushed by the enemy is your luxury repressed. You have missed the profit of your calamity; you have been made most wretched, and you have remained most profligate. (33)

And that you are yet alive is due to God, who spares you that you may be admonished to repent and reform your lives. It is He who has permitted you, ungrateful as you are, to escape the sword of the enemy by calling yourselves His servants, or by finding asylum in the sacred places of the martyrs. (34)

Let these and similar answers—if any fuller and fitter answers can be found—be given to their enemies by the redeemed family of the Lord Christ and by the pilgrim city of King Christ. But let this city bear in mind that among her enemies lie hid those who are destined to be fellow-citizens, that she may not think it a fruitless labour to bear what they inflict as enemies until they become confessors of the faith. So, too, as long as she is a stranger in the world, the city of

God has in her communion, and bound to her by the sacraments, some who shall not eternally dwell in the lot of the saints. Of these, some are now not recognized; others declare themselves and do not hesitate to make common cause with our enemies in murmuring against God, under whose colors they serve. These men you may to-day see thronging the churches with us, to-morrow crowding the theatres of the godless. But we have the less reason to despair of the reclamation even of such persons, if among our most declared enemies there are now some, unknown to themselves, who are destined to become our friends.

In truth, these two cities are entangled together in this world and intermixed until the last judgment effect their separation. I now proceed to speak, as God shall help me, of the rise, progress, and end of these two cities; and what I write, I write for the glory of the city of God, that, being placed in comparison with the other, it may shine with a brighter lustre. (35)

BOOK II

Summary

The Roman gods, celebrated by Roman poets for deeds which would have been punished if committed by Roman citizens, contributed to the degeneration of the empire.

BOOK III

Summary

Just as the Trojan gods did not save Troy, so the Roman gods have not saved Rome from calamities in the past.

BOOK IV

The confusing multitude of pagan gods contributed nothing to the growth of the empire.

*Even if any pagan gods were worth worshipping, it
should not be those who are alleged to give empires
away, but the goddess Felicity—which is not a god,
but a gift of God.*

Is it quite fitting for good men to rejoice in extended empire? After all, it is the iniquity of those with whom just wars
are carried on which favours the growth of a kingdom, which
would certainly still be small if its neighbors, loving peace
and justice, had not by some wrong provoked the carrying
on of war against them; and human affairs being thus more
happy, all kingdoms would be small, rejoicing in neighborly
concord; and thus there would be very many kingdoms of
nations in this world, just as there are very many houses of
citizens in one city. Therefore, to carry on war and to extend
a kingdom over wholly subdued nations seems to bad men to
be felicity, to good men necessity. But because it would be
worse that the injurious should rule over those who are more
righteous, therefore even that is not unsuitably called felicity.
But beyond doubt it is greater felicity to have a good neighbour at peace than to conquer a bad one by making war.

If, therefore, by carrying on wars that were just, and not
impious or unrighteous, the Romans were able to acquire so
great an empire, ought they not to worship as a goddess even
the iniquity of foreigners? For we see that foreign iniquity has
co-operated much in extending the empire by making foreigners so unjust that they became people with whom just
wars might be carried on, with the result that the empire
increased.

9

By these two, therefore, i.e., by foreign injustice and by the goddess Victoria,—for injustice stirs up causes of wars, and Victoria brings these same wars to a happy termination—the empire has increased even while Jove [3] was idle. For what benefits could come from Jove, when things like victory, which might be thought to be his benefits, are held to be gods, called gods, worshipped as gods, and are themselves invoked for these benefits? Or if empire is the gift of Jove, why may not victory also be held to be his gift? And it certainly would have been held to be so, had he been recognized and worshipped as the true King of kings and Lord of lords. (15)

Or do they say, perhaps, that Jupiter sends the goddess Victoria, and that she, as it were, acting in obedience to the king of the gods, comes to those to whom he may have despatched her and takes up her quarters on their side? This is truly said, but not of Jove, whom they, according to their own imagination, feign to be king of the gods, but of Him who is the true eternal King. For He sends, not Victory, who is no person, but His angel, and causes whom He pleases to conquer. And His counsel may be hidden, but it cannot be unjust. (17)

What shall we say, besides, of the idea that Felicity also is a goddess? She has received a temple, she has merited an altar, and suitable rites of worship are paid to her. She alone, then, should be worshipped. (18)

But how does it happen, if Felicity is a goddess, that she herself is not appointed as the only one to be worshipped, since she could confer all things and all at once make men happy? For who wishes anything for any other reason than that he may become happy? Felicity is certainly more valuable than a kingdom. For no one doubts that a man might easily be found who may fear to be a king; but no one is found who is unwilling to be happy. Therefore, if it is thought that the gods can be consulted by augury, or in any other way, the gods themselves should be consulted about whether

[3] Jupiter, the chief divinity of the Romans, whose temple crowned the Capitoline hill.

they may wish to give place to Felicity. If, perchance, the place where a greater and more lofty temple might be built to Felicity should already be occupied by the temples and altars of others, even Jupiter himself might give way, so that Felicity might rather obtain the very pinnacle of the Capitoline hill. For there is not any one who would resist Felicity, except, which is impossible, one who might wish to be unhappy.

The goddess Felicity being thus established in the largest and loftiest place, the citizens should learn whence the furtherance of every good desire should be sought. And so, when by the persuasion of nature herself the superfluous multitude of other gods would have been abandoned, Felicity alone would be worshipped. For who wishes to receive from any god anything else than either felicity or what he supposes to tend to felicity.

But if Felicity is not a goddess, because, as is true, felicity is a gift of God, that God must be sought who has power to give it, and that hurtful multitude of false gods must be abandoned which the vain multitude of foolish men, making gods of the gift of God, follows after. For he cannot be free from infelicity who worships Felicity as a goddess and forsakes God, the giver of felicity; just as he cannot be free from hunger who licks a painted loaf of bread and does not buy it of the man who has a real one. (23)

God, the author and giver of felicity because He alone is the true God, Himself gives earthly kingdoms both to good and bad. And He does not do this rashly and, as it were, fortuitously—for He is God, not fortune—but according to the order of things and times which, though hidden from us, is thoroughly known to Himself. However, He does not serve this order of times as subject to it, but Himself rules and appoints it as Lord and Governor. Felicity He gives only to the good. Whether a man be a subject or a king makes no difference: he may either possess or not possess it. And it shall be full in that life where kings and subjects exist no longer. Earthly kingdoms, however, are given by Him both to the good and to the bad; lest His worshippers, still under the conduct of a very weak mind, should covet these gifts from Him as some great things. (33)

BOOK V

Divine providence and the glory of Rome

The cause of Rome's greatness is divine providence; and providence does not destroy the freedom of the will.

Since, then, it is established that the complete attainment of all we desire is that which constitutes felicity, which is no goddess, but a gift of God, and that therefore men can worship no god save Him who is able to make them happy, let us now consider why God, who is able to give with all other things those good gifts which can be possessed by men who are not good, and consequently not happy, has seen fit to grant such extended and long-continued dominion to the Roman empire. (Preface)

If, following the definition and usage of others, we call those events fortuitous which either have no cause at all or such causes as do not proceed from some intelligible order, and if we say that those events happen by fate which happen independently of the will of God and man by the necessity of a certain order, then the cause of the greatness of the Roman empire is neither fortune nor fate. Human kingdoms, to say it in a word, are established by divine providence. And if any one attributes their existence to fate, because he calls the will or the power of God itself by the name of fate, let him keep his opinion but correct his language. (1)

Cicero, denying that there is any knowledge of future things,[4] maintains with all his might that there is no such knowledge either in God or man.

But, to confess that God exists, and at the same time to deny that He has foreknowledge of future things, is the most

[4] In *De Divinatione*, Book II.

manifest folly. What is it that Cicero feared in the fore-knowledge of future things? Doubtless it was this: if all future events are foreknown, they will happen in the order in which they are foreknown; and if they come to pass in this order, there is a certain order of events foreknown by God; and if a certain order of events is foreknown, then a certain order of causes is foreknown also, for nothing can happen which is not preceded by some efficient cause. But if there is a certain order of causes according to which everything happens which does happen, then by fate, says he, all things happen which do happen. But if this be so, then there is nothing in our own power, and there is no such thing as freedom of will; and if we grant that, says he, the whole economy of life is subverted. In vain are laws enacted. In vain are reproaches, praises, chidings, exhortations had recourse to; and there is no justice whatever in the appointment of rewards for the good and of punishments for the wicked. And that consequences so disgraceful, and absurd, and pernicious to humanity may not follow, Cicero chooses to reject the foreknowledge of future things and places the religious mind into the dilemma of having to make a choice between two things: to say either that some things are in our own power, or that there is foreknowledge—both of which cannot be true; but if the one is affirmed, the other is thereby denied. Being a truly great and wise man, he chose the freedom of the will and denied, in order to confirm this freedom, the foreknowledge of future things; and thus, wishing to make men free, he makes them sacrilegious.

But the religious mind chooses both, confesses both, and maintains both by the faith of piety.

We assert both that God knows all things before they come to pass, and that we do by our free will whatsoever we know and feel to be done by us only because we will it.

That all things come to pass by fate, we do not say. But an order of causes in which the highest efficiency is attributed to the will of God we neither deny nor do we designate it by the name of fate. But it does not follow that, though there is for God a certain order of all causes, there must therefore be nothing depending on the free exercise of our own wills, for our wills themselves are included in that order of causes which is certain to God and which is embraced by His foreknowledge, for human wills are also the causes of human actions; and He who foreknew all the causes of things would certainly among those causes not have been ignorant of our wills. (9)

If we define necessity to be that according to which we say that it is necessary that anything be of such and such a nature, or be done in such and such a manner, I know not why we should have any dread of that necessity taking away the freedom of our will. For we do not put the life of God or the foreknowledge of God under necessity if we should say that it is necessary that God should live for ever and foreknow all things; neither is His power diminished when we say that He cannot die or fall into error—for this is in such a way impossible to Him, that if it were possible for Him, He would be of less power. But assuredly He is rightly called omnipotent, though He can neither die nor fall into error. For He is called omnipotent on account of His doing what He wills, not on account of His suffering what He wills not; for if that should befall Him, He would by no means be omnipotent. Therefore He cannot do some things for the very reason that He is omnipotent. So also, when we say that it is necessary that, when we will, we will by free choice, in so saying we both affirm what is true beyond doubt, and nevertheless do not subject our wills thereby to a necessity which destroys liberty. Our wills, therefore, exist as wills and do themselves whatever we do by willing, and which would not be done if we were unwilling.

It is not the case, therefore, that because God foreknew what would be in the power of our wills, there is for that reason nothing in the power of our wills. For He who foreknew this did not foreknow nothing. Moreover, if He who foreknew what would be in the power of our wills did not foreknow nothing, but something, assuredly, even though He did foreknow, there is something in the power of our wills. Therefore we are by no means compelled, either, retaining the prescience of God, to take away the freedom of the will, or, retaining the freedom of the will, to deny that He is prescient of future things, which is impious. But we embrace both. We faithfully and sincerely confess both. The former, that we may believe well; the latter, that we may live well. For he lives ill who does not believe well concerning God.

Be it therefore far from us, in order to maintain our freedom, to deny the foreknowledge of Him by whose help we are or shall be free. Consequently, it is not in vain that laws are enacted and that reproaches, exhortations, praises, and vituperations are had recourse to; for these also He foreknew, and they are of great avail, even as great as He foreknew that they would be of. Prayers, also, are of avail to procure those things which He foreknew that He would grant to those who offered them; and with justice have rewards been appointed for good deeds, and punishments for sins. For a man does not therefore sin because God foreknew that he would sin. Nay, it cannot be doubted but that it is the man himself who sins when he does sin, because He, whose foreknowledge is infallible, foreknew not that fate, or fortune, or something else would sin, but that the man himself would sin, who, if he wills not, sins not. But if he shall not will to sin, even this did God foreknow. (10)

The empire was given to the Romans by God as a reward for their civic virtues, not by the false gods whom they worshipped.

Let us go on to consider what virtues of the Romans the true God, in whose power are also the kingdoms of the earth, condescended to help in order to raise the empire, and also for what reason He did so.

The ancient and primitive Romans, though their history shows us that, like all the other nations, with the sole exception of the Hebrews, they worshipped false gods and sacrificed victims not to God, but to demons, have nevertheless this commendation bestowed on them by their historian, that they were "greedy of praise, prodigal of wealth, desirous of great glory, and content with a moderate fortune." The same Sallust [5] praises the great men of his own time, Marcus Cato [6] and Caius Caesar, saying that for a long time the republic had no one great in virtue, but that within his memory there had been these two men of eminent virtue and very different pursuits. Now, among the praises which he pronounces on Caesar he put this, that he wished for a great empire, an army, and a new war, that he might have a sphere where his genius and virtue might shine forth. This, forsooth, is what that desire of praise and thirst for glory did. Wherefore, by the love of liberty in the first place, afterwards also by the love of domination and through the desire of praise and glory, they achieved many great things. (12)

But since those Romans were in an earthly city and had before them, as the end of all the offices undertaken in its behalf, its safety, and a kingdom not in heaven but on earth, not in the sphere of eternal life but in the sphere of demise and succession, where the dead are succeeded by the dying, what else but glory should they love, by which they wished even after death to live in the mouths of their admirers? (14)

Now, therefore, with regard to those to whom God did not purpose to give eternal life with His holy angels in His own celestial city, if He had also withheld from them the terrestrial glory of that most excellent empire, a reward would not have been rendered to their virtues by which they sought to attain so great a glory. For as to those who seem to do some good that they may receive glory from men, the Lord also says, "Verily, I say unto you, they have received their reward." (Matt. 6, 2) So also these Romans despised their own private affairs for the sake of the republic, and for its treasury resisted avarice, consulted for the good of their

[5] Sallust, Roman historian living at the time of Caesar (86–34 B.C.). The reference is to *Cat.* VII.

[6] Marcus Porcius Cato Uticensis, 95–46 B.C., a strong opponent of Caesar.

country with a spirit of freedom, addicted neither to what their laws pronounced to be a crime nor to lust. By all these acts, as by the true way, they pressed forward to honors, power, and glory; they were honored among almost all nations; they imposed the laws of their empire upon many nations; and at this day, both in literature and history, they are glorious among almost all nations. There is no reason why they should complain against the justice of the supreme and true God—"they have received their reward." (15)

But the reward of the saints is far different, who even here endured reproaches for that city of God which is hateful to the lovers of this world. That city is eternal. There none are born, for none die. There rises not the sun on the good and the evil, but the Sun of Righteousness protects the good alone. There no great industry shall be expended to enrich the public treasury by suffering privations at home, for there is the common treasury of truth. And therefore it was not only for the sake of recompensing the citizens of Rome that her empire and glory had been so signally extended, but also that the citizens of that eternal city, during their pilgrimage here, might diligently and soberly contemplate these examples and see what a love they owe to the supernal country on account of life eternal, if the terrestrial country was so much beloved by its citizens on account of human glory. (16)

These things being so, we do not attribute the power of giving kingdoms and empires to any save to the true God, who gives happiness in the kingdom of Heaven to the pious alone, but gives kingly power on earth both to the pious and the impious as it may please Him, whose good pleasure is always just. For though we have said something about the principles which guide His administration, in so far as it has seemed good to Him to explain it, nevertheless it is too much for us and far surpasses our strength to discuss the hidden things of men's hearts, and by a clear examination to determine the merits of various kingdoms. He, therefore, who is the one true God, who never leaves the human race without just judgment and help, gave a kingdom to the Romans when

He would, and as great as He would, as He did also to the
Assyrians, and even the Persians. He, I say, gave the Persians
dominion, though they worshipped none of those gods to
whom the Romans believed themselves indebted for the empire. And the same is true in respect of men as well as nations. He who gave power to Augustus gave it also to Nero;
He who gave it to the Christian Constantine [7] gave it also to
the apostate Julian,[8] whose gifted mind was deceived by a
sacrilegious and detestable curiosity, stimulated by the love
of power. (21)

Neither do we say that certain Christian emperors were
therefore happy because they ruled a long time, or, dying a
peaceful death, left their sons to succeed them in the empire,
or subdued the enemies of the republic, or were able both to
guard against and to suppress the attempt of hostile citizens
rising against them. These and other gifts or comforts of this
sorrowful life even certain worshippers of demons have
merited to receive, who do not belong to the kingdom of God
to which these belong; and this is to be traced to the mercy of
God, who would not have those who believe in Him desire
such things as the highest good. But we say that they are
happy if they rule justly, if, more than their own, they love
that kingdom in which they are not afraid to have partners, if
they prefer to govern depraved desires rather than any nation
whatever; and if they do all these things not through ardent
desire of empty glory but through love of eternal felicity, not
neglecting to offer to the true God, who is their God, for
their sins the sacrifices of humility, contrition, and prayer.
Such Christian emperors, we say, are happy in the present
time by hope and are destined to be so in the enjoyment of
the reality itself, when that which we wait for shall have
arrived. (24)

[7] Constantine, sole ruler of the empire from 323–337 A.D., issued in
313 the edict of Milan for the protection of Christians and was himself
baptized shortly before his death.
[8] Julianus Apostata, son of Constantius, the brother of Constantine,
was brought up as a Christian but turned to the teachings of the Neo-
platonists. He was emperor from 361–363 A.D.

BOOK VI

Summary

Disputation against Varro: the pagan gods cannot contribute anything to the happiness of the future life.

BOOK VII

Summary

Eternal life is not obtained by the worship of Jupiter or any other of the more "powerful" gods of the pagans.

BOOK VIII

Philosophy—the love of wisdom—is by definition love of God; and those who follow Plato,
the most eminent of all philosophers, have certain doctrines in common with the Christians.

*Plato and his schools share with the Christians the
knowledge that God is the highest good and that He is
"He who is."*

It is not with ordinary men, but with philosophers that we
must confer concerning the theology which they call natural.
For if Wisdom is God, who made all things, as is attested by
the divine authority and truth, then the philosopher (i.e., a
"lover of wisdom,") is a lover of God. But since the thing
itself which is called wisdom exists not in all who glory in the
name—for it does not follow, of course, that all who are
called philosophers are lovers of true wisdom—we must
needs select from the number of those with whose opininons
we have been able to acquaint ourselves by reading, some
with whom we may not unworthily engage in the treatment
of this question. For I have not in this work undertaken to
refute the vain theological opinions of all the philosophers,
but only of such of them as, agreeing in the belief that there
is a divine nature and that this divine nature is concerned
about human affairs, do nevertheless deny that the worship
of the one unchangeable God is sufficient for the obtaining
of a blessed life after death as well as at the present time, and
hold that, in order to obtain that life, many gods, created, indeed, and appointed to their several spheres by that one God,
are to be worshipped.

These philosophers acknowledge God as the Creator not
only of this visible world, but also of every soul whatsoever;

and they acknowledge God as Him who gives blessedness to the rational soul—of which kind is the human soul—by participation in His own unchangeable and incorporeal light. There is no one who has even a slender knowledge of these little things who does not know of the Platonic philosophers, who derive their name from their master Plato. Concerning this Plato, then, I will briefly state such things as I deem necessary to the present question, mentioning beforehand those who preceded him in the same department of literature. (1)

Socrates is said to have been the first who directed the entire effort of philosophy to the correction and regulation of manners, all who went before him having expended their greatest efforts in the investigation of physical, i.e., natural, phenomena. However, it seems to me that it cannot be certainly discovered whether Socrates did this because he was wearied of obscure and uncertain things, and so wished to direct his mind to the discovery of something manifest and certain, which was necessary in order to obtain a blessed life —that one great object toward which the labour, vigilance, and industry of all philosophers seem to have been directed —or whether, as some yet more favourable to him suppose, he did it because he was unwilling that minds defiled with earthly desires should attempt to raise themselves to divine things. For he saw that human minds search for the causes of things, and, since he believed that the ultimate causes exist nowhere else than in the will of the one true and supreme God, he thought that they could only be comprehended by a purified mind and that therefore all diligence ought to be given to the purification of life by good morals, in order that the mind, delivered from the depressing weight of lusts, might rise by its native vigour to eternal things and, with purified understanding, contemplate that nature which is incorporeal and unchangeable light, where live the causes of all created natures.

Illustrious both in his life and in his death, Socrates left very many disciples of his philosophy who vied with one another in desire for proficiency in handling those moral questions which concern the chief good (summum bonum), the possession of which can make a man blessed; and because, in the disputations of Socrates, it did not evidently appear what he held to be the chief good, every one took from these disputations what pleased him best, and every one placed the final good in whatever it appeared to him to consist.

Now the final good is that by which he who attains it is blessed. But so diverse were the opinions held by those followers of Socrates concerning this final good, that some placed the chief good in pleasure, others in virtue; others, again, thought otherwise, and it would be too tedious to recount all the various opinions. (3)

But, among the disciples of Socrates, Plato was the one who shone with a glory which far excelled that of the others and who not unjustly eclipsed them all. Those who are praised as having most closely followed Plato—who is justly preferred to all the other philosophers of the Gentiles—and who are said to have manifested the greatest acuteness in understanding him, do perhaps entertain such an idea of God as to admit that in Him are to be found the cause of existence, the ultimate reason for the understanding, and the end in reference to which the whole life is to be regulated. For if man has been so created that he may attain through that which is most excellent in him to that which excels all things —i.e., to the one true God, without whom no nature exists, no teaching instructs, and no exercise profits—then let Him be sought in whom all things are secure to us, let Him be discovered in whom all truth becomes certain to us, let Him be loved in whom all becomes right to us. (4)

If, then, Plato defined the wise man as one who imitates, knows, and loves this God, and who is rendered blessed through fellowship with Him in His own blessedness, why discuss with the other philosophers? It is evident that none come nearer to us than the Platonists. (5)

These philosophers have seen that no material body is God, and therefore they have transcended all bodies in seek-

ing for God. They have seen that whatever is changeable is
not the most high God, and therefore they have transcended
every soul and all changeable spirits in seeking the supreme.
They have seen also that, in every changeable thing, the
form [9] which makes it that which it is, whatever be its mode
or nature, can only exist through Him who truly is, because
He is unchangeable. And therefore, whether we consider the
whole body of the world, its figure, qualities, and orderly
movement, and also all the bodies which are in it; or whether
we consider all life, either that which nourishes and subsists,
as the life of trees, or that which, besides this, has also sensa-
tion, as the life of beasts; or that which adds to all these intelligence, as the life of man; or that which does not need the
support of nutriment, but only subsists, feels, and under-
stands, as the life of the angels—all can only exist through
Him who absolutely is. For to Him it is not one thing to be
and another to live, as though he could be, not living; nor is
it to Him one thing to live and another thing to understand,
as though He could live, not understanding; nor is it to Him
one thing to understand, another thing to be blessed, as
though He could understand and not be blessed. But to Him
to live, to understand, to be blessed, are to be. And the
Platonists have understood, from this unchangeableness and
this simplicity, that all things must have been made by Him,
and that He could Himself have been made by none. (6)

Plato determined the final good to be to live according to
virtue and affirmed that he only can attain to virtue who
knows and imitates God—which knowledge and imitation
are the only causes of blessedness. Therefore he did not
doubt that to philosophize is to love God, whose nature is
incorporeal. Whence it certainly follows that the student of
wisdom, that is, the philosopher, will then become blessed
when he shall have begun to enjoy God. For though he who
enjoys that which he loves is not necessarily blessed—for
many are miserable by loving that which ought not to be
loved, and still more miserable when they enjoy it—never-

[9] Lat.: species.

theless no one is blessed who does not enjoy that which he loves. For even they who love things which ought not to be loved do not count themselves blessed by loving merely, but by enjoying them. Who, then, but the most miserable will deny that he is blessed who enjoys what he loves when he loves the true and highest good? But the true and highest good, according to Plato, is God; and therefore Plato calls him a philosopher who loves God; for philosophy is directed to the obtaining of the blessed life, and he who loves God is blessed in the enjoyment of God. (8)

But no matter who were the philosophers who thought that the supreme God is both the maker of all created things, the light by which things are known, and the good in reference to which things are to be done; that we have in Him the first principle of nature, the truth of the doctrine, and the happiness of life—whether these philosophers are, rather fittingly, called Platonists, or whether they may give some other name to their sect—we prefer these to all other philosophers and confess that they approach nearest to us. (9)

Certain partakers with us in the grace of Christ wonder when they hear and read that Plato had conceptions concerning God in which they recognize considerable agreement with the truth of our religion. The most striking thing in this connection is the answer which was given to the question elicited from the holy Moses. For, when Moses asked what was the name of that God who was commanding him to go and deliver the Hebrew people out of Egypt, this answer was given: "I am He who is; and thou shalt say to the children of Israel, 'He who *is* sent me unto you!' " (Ex. 3, 14)—as if, compared with Him who truly *is* because He is unchangeable, those things which have been created mutable *are* not, a truth which Plato vehemently held and most diligently commended. And I know not whether this insight is anywhere to be found in the books of those who were before Plato, unless in that book where it is said, "I am He who is; and thou shalt say to the children of Israel, 'He who is sent me unto you!' " (11)

But we need not determine from what source Plato learned these things, whether it was from the books of the ancients who preceded him, or, as is more likely, from the words of the apostle: "Because that which is known of God has been manifested among them, for God hath manifested it to them. For His invisible things from the creation of the world are clearly seen, being understood by those things which have been made, also His eternal power and Godhead." (Rom. 1, 20) (12)

The Christians honour their martyrs, but they worship only God.

With such blindness do impious men, as it were, stumble over mountains and will not see the things which strike their own eyes, that they do not attend to the fact that in all the literature of the pagans there are not found any, or scarcely any gods, who have not been men to whom, when dead, divine honours have been paid. (26)

We Christians do not build temples and ordain priests, rites, and sacrifices for martyrs; for martyrs are not our gods, but their God is our God. Certainly we honour their reliquaries as the memorials of holy men of God who strove for the truth even to the death of their bodies so that the true religion might be made known and false and fictitious religion exposed. But who ever heard a priest of the faithful, standing at an altar built for the honour and worship of God over the holy body of some martyr, say in the prayers, "I offer to thee a sacrifice, O Peter, or O Paul, or O Cyprian?" for it is to God that sacrifices are offered at their tombs—to that God who made them both men and martyrs and who associated them with holy angels in celestial honour. And the reason why we pay such honours to their memory is that, by so doing, we may both give thanks to the true God for their victories and that, by recalling them afresh to remembrance, we may stir ourselves up to imitate them by seeking to obtain like crowns and palms, calling to our help that same God on whom they called. Therefore, whatever honours the religious may pay in the places of martyrs, they are but honours rendered to their memory, not sacred rites or sacrifices offered to dead men as to gods. (27)

BOOK IX

Summary

To Christ alone belongs the office of providing men with eternal blessedness.

BOOK X

The angels do not desire us to worship them but
God, for we and they together are the one
city of God.

*The only sacrifice acceptable to God is a life sacri-
ficed, i.e., made holy, so that we may be blessed by
being united to God.*

It is the decided opinion of all who use their brains, that
all men desire to be happy. But who are happy, or how they
become so, these are questions about which the weakness of
human understanding stirs endless and angry controversies
in which philosophers have wasted their strength and expended their leisure.

The Platonists had the wit to perceive that the human soul,
immortal and rational or intellectual as it is, cannot be happy
except by partaking of the light of that God by whom both
itself and the world were made; and also that the happy life
which all men desire cannot be reached by any who does not
cleave with a pure and holy love to that one supreme good,
the unchangeable God. But as even these philosophers,
whether accommodating to the folly and ignorance of the
people, or, as the apostle says, "becoming vain in their
imaginations," (Rom. 1, 21) supposed or allowed others to
suppose that many gods should be worshipped, so that some
of them considered that divine honour by worship and sacrifice should be rendered even to the demons, we must now, by
God's help, ascertain what is thought about our religious
worship and piety by those immortal and blessed spirits who
dwell in the heavenly places and whom the Platonists call
gods, and some either good demons, or, like us, angels. To
put it more plainly, we must ascertain whether the angels

29

desire us to offer sacrifice and worship and to consecrate our possessions and ourselves to them, or only to God, theirs and ours. (1)

Our good is nothing else than to be united to God. It is, if I may say so, by spiritually embracing Him that the intellectual soul is filled and impregnated with true virtues. We are enjoined to love this good with all our heart, with all our soul, with all our strength.

To this good we ought to be led by those who love us, and to lead those we love. Thus are fulfilled those two commandments on which hang all the law and the prophets: "Thou shalt love the Lord thy God with all thy heart, and with all thy mind, and with all thy soul"; and "Thou shalt love thy neighbour as thyself." (Matt. 22, 37–40)

For, that man might be intelligent in his self-love, there was appointed for him an end to which he might refer all his actions, that he might be blessed. For he who loves himself wishes nothing else than this. And the end set before him is "to draw near to God." And so, when one who has this intelligent self-love is commanded to love his neighbour as himself, what else is enjoined than that he shall do all in his power to commend to him the love of God? This is the worship of God, this is true religion, this right piety, this the service due to God only. If any immortal power, then, no matter with what virtue endowed, loves us as himself, he must desire that we find our happiness by submitting ourselves to Him in submission to whom he himself finds happiness. If he does not worship God, he is wretched because deprived of God; if he worships God, he cannot wish to be worshipped in God's stead. On the contrary, these higher powers acquiesce heartily in the divine sentence in which it is written, "He that sacrificeth unto any god, save unto the Lord only, he shall be utterly destroyed." (Ex. 22, 20) (3)

And who is so foolish as to suppose that the things offered to God are needed by Him for some uses of His own? Divine Scripture in many places explodes this idea. Not to be wearisome, suffice it to quote this brief saying from a psalm: "I have said to the Lord, Thou art my God: for Thou needest not my goodness." (Ps. 16, 2) We must believe, then, that God has no need of man's righteousness and that whatever right worship is paid to God profits not Him, but man. For no man would say he did a benefit to a fountain by drinking, or to the light by seeing. And the fact that the ancient church offered animal sacrifices, which the people of God now-a-days read of without imitating, proves nothing else than that those sacrifices signified the things which we do for the purpose of drawing near to God and of inducing our neighbour to do the same. A sacrifice, therefore, is the visible sacrament or sacred sign of an invisible sacrifice. Hence that penitent in the psalm, entreating God to be merciful to his sins, says, "If Thou desiredst sacrifice, I would give it: Thou delightest not in whole burnt-offerings. The sacrifice of God is a broken heart: a heart contrite and humble God will not despise." (Ps. 51, 16–17) Observe how, in the very words in which he is expressing God's refusal of sacrifice, he shows that God requires sacrifice. He does not desire the sacrifice of a slaughtered beast, but He desires the sacrifice of a contrite heart. (5)

A true sacrifice is every work which is done that we may be united to God in holy fellowship, a work which has a reference to that supreme good and end in which alone we can be truly blessed.

Thus man himself, consecrated in the name of God and vowed to God, is a sacrifice in so far as he dies to the world that he may live in God. For this is a part of that mercy which each man shows to himself; as it is written, "Have mercy on thy soul by pleasing God." (Rom. 6, 13)

Since, therefore, true sacrifices are works of mercy to ourselves or others, done with a reference to God, and since works of mercy have no other object than the relief of distress or the conferring of happiness, and since there is no happiness apart from that good of which it is said, "It is good for me to be very near to God," it follows that the whole redeemed city, that is to say, the congregation or community of the saints, is offered to God as our sacrifice through the great High Priest, who offered Himself to God in His passion for us, that we might be members of this glorious head according to the form of a servant. For it was this form He offered, in this He was offered, because it is according to it He is Mediator, in this He is our Priest, in this the Sacrifice.

This is the sacrifice of Christians: we, being many, are one body in Christ. And this also is the sacrifice which the Church continually celebrates in the sacrament of the altar, known to the faithful, in which she teaches that she herself is offered in the offering she makes to God. (6)

The angels do not wish to be worshipped.

Since these blessed and immortal spirits who inhabit celestial dwellings and rejoice in the communications of their Creator's fulness—firm in His eternity, assured in His truth, holy by His grace—compassionately and tenderly regard us miserable mortals and wish us to become immortal and happy, it is very right that they do not desire us to sacrifice to themselves, but to Him whose sacrifice they know themselves to be in common with us. For we and they together are the one city of God, to which it is said in the psalm, "Glorious things are spoken of thee, O city of God"; (Ps. 87, 3) the human part sojourning here below, the angelic aiding from above. (7)

BOOK XI

The origin of the two cities

The author promises to trace the origin of the two cities back to their beginning: to the moment when the bad angels, shortly after their creation, were separated from the good angels.

The city of God we speak of is the same to which testimony is borne by that Scripture, which excels all the writings of all nations by its divine authority and has brought under its influence all kinds of minds, and this not by the chance decisions of human minds, but obviously by an express providential arrangement. For there it is written, "Glorious things are spoken of the, O city of God." (Ps. 87, 3) And in another psalm we read, "There is a river, the streams whereof shall make glad the city of God, the holy place of the tabernacles of the Most High. God is in the midst of her, she shall not be moved." (Ps. 46, 4–5) From these and similar testimonies, all of which it were tedious to cite, we have learned that there is a city of God; and its Founder has inspired us with a love which makes us covet its citizenship.

Now, recognizing what is expected of me, I will endeavour to treat of the origin, history, and deserved destinies of the two cities, i.e., of the earthly and of the heavenly city, which, as we said, are in this present world commingled and, as it were, entangled together. And, first, I will explain how these two cities began with the difference that arose among the angels. (1)

The two cities can not be traced back further, because time itself began with creation.

33

Of all visible things, the world is the greatest; of all invisible, the greatest is God. But, that the world is, we see; that God is, we believe. That God made the world, we can believe from no one more safely than from God Himself. But where have we heard Him? Nowhere more distinctly than in the Holy Scriptures, where His prophet said, "In the beginning God created the heavens and the earth." (Gen. 1, 1)

But why did God choose then to create the heavens and the earth which He had not made up to that time? (4) We must see what reply can be made to those who agree that God is the Creator of the world, but who nevertheless have difficulties about the time of its creation. (5)

If eternity and time are rightly distinguished by this, that time does not exist without some change, while in eternity there is no change, who does not see that there could have been no time had not some creature been made which by some motion could give birth to change, so that, since the various phases of such motion and change cannot be simultaneous but must succeed one another, time would begin in these shorter or longer intervals of duration? Since then, God, in whose eternity is no change at all, is the Creator and Ordainer of time, I do not see how He can be said to have created the world after spaces of time had elapsed, unless it be said that prior to the world there was some creature by whose movement time could pass. And if the sacred and infallible Scriptures say that God created the heavens and the earth in the beginning, in order that it may be understood that He made nothing previously—for if He had made anything before the rest, this thing would rather be said to have been made "in the beginning"—then assuredly the world was made, not in time, but simultaneously with time. (6)

Both the good angels and the bad ones existed before the stars were made.

At present, since I have undertaken to treat of the origin of the holy city, and first of the holy angels, who constitute a large part of this city, and indeed the more blessed part, since they have never been expatriated, I will give myself to the task of explaining, with God's help, and as far as seems suitable, the Scriptures which relate to this point.

Where Scripture speaks of the world's creation, it is not plainly said whether or when the angels were created. But if mention of them is made, it is made implicitly under the name of "heaven," when it is said, "In the beginning God created the heavens and the earth," or perhaps rather under the name of "light." Who, then, will be bold enough to suggest that the angels were made after the six days' creation? If anyone is so foolish, his folly is disposed of by a scripture passage of like authority where God says, "When the stars were made, all my angels praised me with a loud voice." (Job 38, 7) The angels therefore existed before the stars, and if we are justified in understanding by "light," when we read "God said, 'Let there be light,' and there was light," (Gen. 1, 3) the creation of the angels, then certainly they were created partakers of the eternal light which is the unchangeable Wisdom of God. (9)

Probably, both groups of angels were at first on an equal footing: they enjoyed a life not yet blessed; for blessedness includes awareness of permanence.

Yet the angels were not so created in order that they might exist and live in any way whatever, but they were enlightened that they might live wisely and blessedly.

Some of them, having turned away from this light, have not won this wise and blessed life which is certainly eternal and accompanied with the sure confidence of its eternity; but they have still the life of reason, though darkened with folly, and this they cannot lose even if they would. Wherefore, although everything eternal is not therefore blessed—for hellfire is eternal—yet if no life can be truly and perfectly blessed except it be eternal, the life of these angels was not blessed, for it was doomed to end and therefore not eternal whether they knew it or not. (11)

From all this, it will readily occur to anyone that the blessedness which an intelligent being desires as its legitimate object results from a combination of these two things, namely, that it uninterruptedly enjoy the unchangeable good, which is God; and that it be delivered from all doubt and know with certainty that it shall eternally abide in the same enjoyment. That it is so with the angels of light we piously believe; but that the fallen angels, who by their own default lost that light, did not enjoy this blessedness even before they sinned, reason bids us conclude. Yet if their life was of any duration before they fell, we must allow them a blessedness of some kind, though not that which is accompanied with foresight. But if it seems hard to believe that, when the angels were created, they were not all from the beginning on an equal footing until those who are now evil did of their own will fall away from the light of goodness, it is certainly much harder to believe that the holy angels are now uncertain of their eternal blessedness. It follows either that the angels were unequal or that, if equal, the good angels were assured of the eternity of their blessedness after the perdition of the others; unless, possibly, some one may say that the words of the Lord about the devil, "He was a murderer from the beginning, and abode not in the truth," (John 8, 44) are to be understood to mean that he was not only a murderer from the beginning of the human race, when man, whom he could kill by his deceit, was made, but also that he did not abide in the truth from the time of his own creation and was accordingly never blessed with the holy angels, but refused to submit to his Creator and proudly exulted as if in a private lordship of his own, and was thus deceived and deceiving. For the dominion of the Almighty cannot be eluded; and he who will not piously submit himself to things as they are, proudly feigns, and mocks himself with a state of things that does not exist. (13)

The separation of the good angels from the bad—and
thereby the foundation of the two cities—was effected,
before the fall of the bad angels, by separating the
"light" from "darkness."

To me it does not seem incongruous with the working of God, if we understand that the angels were created when the first "light" was made, and that a separation was made between the holy and the unclean angels when "God divided the light from the darkness; and God called the light Day, and the darkness He called Night." (Gen. 1, 3–4) For He alone could make this discrimination who was able also, before they fell, to foreknow that they would fall and that, being deprived of the light of truth, they would abide in the darkness of pride. For, so far as regards that physical day and night with which we are familiar, He commanded those luminaries of heaven that are obvious to our senses to divide between the light and the darkness. "Let there be," He says, "lights in the firmament of the heaven, to divide the day from the night"; (Gen. 1, 14) and shortly afterwards He says, "And God made two great lights; the greater light to rule the day, and the lesser light to rule the night: He made the stars also. And God set them in the firmament of the heaven, to give light upon the earth, and to rule over the day and over the night, and to divide the light from the darkness." (Gen. 1, 14–18) But between that "light" which is the holy company of the angels spiritually radiant with the illumination of the truth, and that opposing "darkness" which is the noisome foulness of the spiritual condition of those angels who are turned away from the light of righteousness, only He Himself could divide from whom their wickedness (not of nature, but of will), while yet it was future, could not be hidden or uncertain. (19)

As created by God, all the angels were good, i.e. re-
sembling the supreme Good, God, who had made them.

Then, we must not pass from this passage of Scripture

without noticing that when "God said, 'Let there be light!'
and there was light," it was immediately added, "And God
saw the light, that it was good." (Gen. 1, 4) No such expression followed the statement that He separated the "light"
from the "darkness" and called the "light" Day and the
"darkness" Night, lest the seal of His approval might seem to
be set on such "darkness," as well as on the "light." For
when the darkness was not subject of disapprobation, as
when it was divided by the heavenly bodies from this light
which our eyes discern, the statement that God saw that it
was good is inserted not before, but after the division is recorded. "And God set them," so runs the passage, "in the
firmament of the heaven to give light upon the earth, and to
rule over the day and over the night, and to divide the light
from the darkness: and God saw that it was good." (Gen. 1,
17–18) For He approved of both, because both were sinless.
But where God said, " 'Let there be light!' and there was
light; and God saw the light, that it was good"; (Gen. 1,
3–4) and the narrative goes on, "and God divided the light
from the darkness: and God called the light Day, and the
darkness He called Night," (Gen. 1, 4–5) there was not in
this place subjoined the statement, "And God saw that it was
good," lest both should be designated good, while one of
them was evil, not by nature, but by its own fault. And
therefore, in this case, the "light" alone received the approba-
tion of the Creator, while the angelic "darkness," though it
had been ordained, was not approved. (20)

For what else is to be understood by that invariable re-
frain, "And God saw that it was good," than the approval of
the work in its design, which is the wisdom of God? For certainly God did not in the actual achievement of the work first
learn that it was good, but, on the contrary, nothing would
have been made had it not been first known by Him. While,
therefore, He sees that that is good which, had He not seen
it before it was made, would never have been made, it is plain
that He is not discovering, but teaching that it is good. It is
not as if the knowledge of God were of various kinds, know-

ing in different ways things which as yet are not, things which are, and things which have been. For not in our fashion does He look forward to what is future, nor at what is present, nor back upon what is past; but in a manner quite different and far and profoundly remote from our way of thinking. For He does not pass from this to that by transition of thought, but beholds all things with absolute unchangeableness; so that of those things which emerge in time, the things of the future, indeed, are not yet, and the present are now, and the past no longer are; but all of these are by Him comprehended in His stable and eternal presence. Neither does He see in one fashion by the eye, in another by the mind, for He is not composed of mind and body; nor does His present knowledge differ from that which it ever was or shall be, for those variations of time, past, present, and future, though they alter our knowledge, do not affect His, "with whom is no variableness, neither shadow of turning." (James 1, 17) Neither is there any growth from thought to thought in the conceptions of Him in whose spiritual vision all things which He knows are at once embraced. For as without any movement that time can measure, He Himself moves all temporal things, so He knows all times with a knowledge that time cannot measure. And therefore He saw that what He had made was good, when He saw that it was good to make it. And when He saw it made, He had not on that account a twofold nor an in any way increased knowledge of it, as if He had less knowledge before He made what He saw. For certainly He would not be the perfect worker He is, unless His knowledge were so perfect as to receive no addition from His finished works. Wherefore, if the only object had been to inform us who made the light, it had been enough to say, "God made the light"; and if further information regarding the means by which it was made had been intended, it would have sufficed to say, "And God said, 'Let there be light!' and there was light," that we might know not only that God had made the world, but also that He had made it by the word. But because it was right that three leading truths regarding

the creature be intimated to us, namely, who made it, by
what means, and why, it is written, "God said, 'Let there be
light!' and there was light. And God saw the light, that it
was good." If, then, we ask who made it, it was "God." If,
by what means, He said "Let it be!" and it was. If we ask,
why He made it, "it was good." Neither is there any author
more excellent than God, nor any skill more efficacious than
the word of God, nor any cause better than that good might
be created by the good God. (21)

We believe, we maintain, we faithfully preach, that the
Father begat the Word, that is, Wisdom, by which all things
were made, the only-begotten Son, one as the Father is one,
eternal as the Father is eternal, and, equally with the Father,
supremely good; and that the Holy Spirit is the Spirit alike
of Father and Son, and is Himself consubstantial and co-
eternal with both; and that this whole is a Trinity by reason
of the individuality of the persons, and one God by reason of
the indivisible divine substance. It is the Father of the Word
who said "Let there be." And that which was made when He
spoke was certainly made by means of the Word. And by the
words, "God saw that it was good," (Gen. 1, 10) it is sufficiently intimated that God made what was made not from
any necessity, nor for the sake of supplying any want, but
solely from His own goodness, i.e., because it was good. And
this is stated after the creation had taken place, that there
might be no doubt that the thing made satisfied the goodness
on account of which it was made. (24)

*Even in ourselves we recognize a great good: the image
of the Trinity; for we exist, we know, and we love.*

And we indeed recognize in ourselves the image of God,
that is, of the supreme Trinity, an image which, though it be
not equal to God, or rather, though it be very far removed
from Him—being neither co-eternal, nor, to say all in a
word, consubstantial with Him—is yet nearer to Him in nature than any other of His works, and is destined to be yet

restored, that it may bear a still closer resemblance. For we both are and know that we are, and we delight in our being and in our knowledge of it. And about these three things no true-seeming error disturbs us; for I am most certain that I am, that I know it, and that I delight in it. In respect of these truths, I am not at all afraid of the arguments of the Academicians, who say, What if you are deceived? For if I am deceived, I am. For he who is not, cannot be deceived; and if I am deceived, by this same token I am. And since I am if I am deceived, how am I deceived in believing that I am? For it is certain that I am if I am deceived. Since, therefore, I, the person deceived, should exist, even if I were deceived, certainly I am not deceived in this knowledge that I am. And, consequently, neither am I deceived in knowing that I know. For, as I know that I am, so I know also that I know. And when I love these two things, I add to them a certain third thing, namely, my love, which is of equal moment. For neither am I deceived in this, that I love, since in those things which I love I am not deceived; though even if these were false, it would still be true that I *loved* false things. (26)

And how much human nature loves knowledge, and how it shrinks from being deceived, will be sufficiently understood from the fact that every man prefers to grieve in a sane mind rather than to be glad in madness. And this grand and wonderful power of knowledge belongs to men alone of all animals; for, though some of them have keener eyesight than ourselves for this world's light, they cannot attain to that spiritual light with which our mind is somehow irradiated, so that we can form right judgments of all things. The outward forms (of material things), which lend beauty to this visible structure of the world, are perceived by our senses, so that these material things seem to wish to compensate for their own want of knowledge by providing us with knowledge. But we perceive them by our bodily senses in such a way that we do not judge of them by these senses. For we have another and far superior sense, belonging to the inner man, by which we perceive what things are just, and what

unjust—just by means of an intelligible idea, unjust by the
want of it. By this inner sense I am assured both that I am,
and that I know this; and these two I love, and in the same
manner I am assured that I love them. (27)

The holy angels share in God's life and thought and
are assured of eternal blessedness.

But in this book let us go on as we have begun, with God's
help, to speak of the city of God, not in its state of pilgrimage
and mortality, but as it exists ever immortal in the heavens
—that is, let us speak of the holy angels who maintain their
allegiance to God, who never were, nor ever shall be, apostate, between whom and those who forsook light eternal and
became darkness, God, as we have already said, made at
first a separation. (28)

Those holy angels come to the knowledge of God not by
audible words, but by the presence to their souls of immutable truth, i.e., of the only-begotten Word of God; and
they know this Word Himself, and the Father, and their Holy
Spirit, and that this Trinity is indivisible, and that the three
persons of it are one substance, and that there are not three
Gods but one God; and this they so know that it is better understood by them than we are by ourselves. Thus, too, they
know the creature also, not in itself, but by this better way,
in the wisdom of God, as if in the art by which it was created; and, consequently, they know themselves better in God
than in themselves, though they also have this latter knowledge. For there is a great difference between knowing a thing
in the design in conformity to which it was made, and
knowing it in itself—e.g., the straightness of lines and cor-
rectness of figures is known in one way when mentally conceived, in another when described on paper. (29)

At the same time, let none doubt that the holy angels in
their heavenly abodes are, though not, indeed, co-eternal
with God, yet secure and certain of eternal and true felicity.
To their company the Lord teaches that His little ones be-

long; and not only says, "They shall be equal to the angels of God," (Matt. 22, 30) but shows, too, what blessed contemplation the angels themselves enjoy, saying, "Take heed that ye despise not one of these little ones: for I say unto you, that in heaven their angels do always behold the face of my Father which is in Heaven." (Matt. 18, 10) (32)

That certain angels sinned and were thrust down to the lowest parts of this world, where they are, as it were, incarcerated till their final damnation in the day of judgment, the Apostle Peter plainly declares when he says that "God spared not the angels that sinned, but cast them down to hell, and delivered them into chains of darkness to be reserved unto judgment." (2. Peter 2, 4) Who, then, can doubt that God, either in foreknowledge or in act, separated between these and the rest?

These two angelic communities, then, dissimilar and contrary to one another, the one both by nature good and by will upright, the other also good by nature but by will depraved, are spoken of in Genesis under the names of "light" and "darkness." (33)

BOOK XII

The difference between blessedness and wretchedness is a difference in the "amplitude" of being, and the wicked angels became wretched by turning from the highest good to a lower good.

The blessedness of the good angels consists in the amplitude of existence which they enjoy by adhering to God. The wretchedness of the wicked angels is the reduced amplitude of existence which they suffer by not having adhered to God.

It has already in the preceding book been shown how the two cities originated among the angels. Before I speak of the creation of man, and show how the cities took their rise so far as regards the race of rational mortals, I see that I must first, so far as I can, adduce what may demonstrate that it is not incongruous and unsuitable to speak of a society composed of angels and men together; so that there are not four cities or societies—two, namely, of angels, and as many of men—but rather two in all, one composed of the good, the other of the wicked, angels or men indifferently.

That the contrary propensities in good and bad angels have arisen, not from a difference in their nature and origin, since God, the good Author and Creator of all essences, created them both, but from a difference in their wills and desires, it is impossible to doubt. While some angels steadfastly continued in that which was the common good of all, namely, in God Himself, others, being enamoured rather of their own power, as if they could be their own good, lapsed to this private good of their own. The cause, therefore, of the blessedness of the good is adherence to God. And so the cause of the others' misery will be found in the contrary, that is, in their not adhering to God. Wherefore, if, when the question is asked, why are the former blessed, it is rightly answered, because they adhere to God; and if, when it is asked, why are the latter miserable, it is rightly answered, because they do not adhere to God, then there is no other good for the rational or intellectual creature save God only. Thus, though it is not every creature that can be blessed—for beasts, trees, stones, and things of that kind have not this capacity—yet those creatures who have that capacity cannot be blessed of themselves—for they have been created out of nothing—but only by Him who created them. For they are blessed by the possession of that whose loss makes them miserable. God, then, who is blessed not in another, but in Himself, cannot be miserable, because He cannot lose Himself.

Accordingly we say that there is no unchangeable good but the one, true, blessed God; that the things which He made are indeed good because from Him, yet mutable because made not out of Him, but out of nothing. Yet those mutable things which can adhere to the immutable good and so be blessed, are very good, although they are not the supreme good, for God is a greater good; for so completely is He their good that without Him they cannot but be wretched. And the other things in the universe are not better on this account, that they cannot be miserable. But as the sentient nature, even when it feels pain, is superior to the stony, which can feel none, so the rational nature, even when it is wretched, is more excellent than that which lacks reason or feeling and can therefore experience no misery. And since this is so, then for this rational nature, which has been created so excellent that, though mutable itself, it can secure its blessedness by adhering to the immutable good—for it will not be satisfied unless it be perfectly blessed, and cannot be thus blessed save in God—for this nature, I say, not to adhere to God is manifestly a fault. Now every fault injures a nature and is consequently contrary to that nature. The creature, therefore, which cleaves to God, differs from those who fail to, fail not by nature but by fault; and yet by this very fault the nature itself is proved to be very noble and admirable. For that nature is certainly praised, the fault of which is justly blamed, as when we say that blindness is a defect of the eyes, we prove that sight belongs to the nature of the eyes. And thus, since every fault is an injury of the nature, that very fault of the wicked angels, their departure from God, is sufficient proof that God created their nature so good that it is an injury not to be with God. (1)

This may be enough to prevent any one from supposing, when we speak of the apostate angels, that they had a nature different from that of the others, a nature derived, as it were, from some different origin, and not from God. From the great impiety of this error we shall disentangle ourselves the more readily and easily, the more distinctly we understand that which God spoke by the angel when He sent Moses to the children of Israel: "I am He who is." (Exod. 3, 14) For since God is the supreme existence, that is to say, since He supremely is and is therefore unchangeable, He gave to the things He made being, but not that supreme being which He Himself is. To some He communicated a more ample, to others a more limited existence, and thus arranged the natures of beings in ranks. (2)

All natures, then, inasmuch as they are, and have therefore a rank and species of their own, and a kind of internal harmony, are certainly good. And when they are in the places assigned to them by the order of their nature, they preserve such being as they have received. (5)

Thus the true cause of the blessedness of the good angels is found to be this, that they cleave to Him who supremely is. And if we ask the cause of the misery of the bad, it occurs to us, and not unreasonably, that they are miserable because they have forsaken Him who supremely is, and have turned to themselves who have no supreme existence. And as adherence to God was the condition of their enjoying an ampler being, they diminished it by preferring themselves to Him. This was the first defect, and the first impoverishment, and the first flaw of their nature, a nature which was created, not indeed supremely existent, but finding its blessedness in the enjoyment of the Supreme Being; whilst by abandoning Him this nature should become, not indeed no nature at all, but a nature with a less ample existence and therefore wretched.

When the wicked angels turned their wills (i.e., their love) from a greater to a lower good, they did so by a free, spontaneous act.

If the further question be asked, "What was the efficient cause of their evil will?" there is none. For what is it which makes the will bad, when it is the will itself which makes the action bad? And consequently a bad will is the cause of bad actions, but nothing is the cause of a bad will. For when the will abandons what is above itself and turns to what is lower, it becomes evil—not because that is evil to which it turns, but because the turning itself is wicked. (6)

I know likewise that the will could not become evil, were it unwilling to become so; and therefore its failings are justly punished, being not necessary but voluntary. For its defection is not to evil things, that is to say, not towards things that are naturally and in themselves evil, but the defection of the will is evil because it wills contrary to the order of nature, abandoning that which has supreme being for that which has less. For avarice is not a fault inherent in gold, but in the man who inordinately loves gold to the detriment of justice, which ought to be held in incomparably higher regard than gold. Consequently he who inordinately loves the good which any nature possesses, even though he obtain it, himself becomes evil in the good, and wretched because deprived of a greater good. (8)

And thus we are driven to believe that the holy angels never existed without a good will or the love of God. But the angels who, though created good, are nevertheless evil now, became so by their own evil will. And a will cannot be made evil by a good nature, unless there is a voluntary defection from good; for not good, but a defection from good, is the cause of evil. These angels, therefore, either received less of the grace of the divine love than those who persevered in the same; or if both were created equally good, then, while the one fell by their evil will, the others were more abundantly assisted, and attained to that pitch of blessedness at which they became certain they should never fall from it—as we have already shown in the preceding book. We must therefore acknowledge, with the praise due to the Creator, that not only of men, but primarily and principally of angels it is true, as it is written, "It is good to draw near to God." (Ps. 73. 28) And those who have this good in common, have, both with Him to whom they draw near and with one another a holy fellowship, and form one city of God. And I see that, as I have now spoken of the rise of this city among the angels, it is time to speak of the origin of that part of it which is hereafter to be united to the immortal angels, and which at present is being gathered from among mortal men. (9)

God, though creating man in such a way that the unity of human society should seem desirable to men, nevertheless knew that mankind, too, would eventually form two opposed societies.

Who can search out the unsearchable depth of this purpose, who can scrutinize the inscrutable wisdom wherewith God, without change of will, created man, who had never before been, and gave him an existence in time, and increased the human race from one individual? (14)

And God was not ignorant that man would sin and that being himself made subject now to death, he would propagate men doomed to die, and that these mortals would run to such enormities in sin that even the beasts devoid of rational will would live more securely and peaceably with their own kind than men, who had been propagated from one individual for the very purpose of commending concord. For not even lions or dragons have ever waged with their kind such wars as men have waged with one another. But God foresaw also that by His grace a people would be called to adoption and that they, being justified by the remission of their sins, would be united by the Holy Ghost to the holy angels. (22)

Among the terrestrial animals man was made by Him in His own image, and, for the reason I have given, was made one individual, though he was not left solitary. For there is nothing so social by nature, so unsocial by its corruption, as this race. And human nature has nothing more appropriate, either for the prevention of discord or for the healing of it where it exists, than the remembrance of that first parent of us all, whom God was pleased to create alone that all men might be derived from one, and that they might thus be admonished to preserve unity among their whole multitude.

But at present, since this book must be concluded, let us merely say that in this first man, who was created in the beginning, there was laid the foundation, not indeed evidently, but in God's foreknowledge, of these two cities or societies, so far as regards the human race. For from that man all men were to be derived—some of them to be associated with the good angels in their reward, others with the wicked in punishment. (27)

BOOK XIII

Death is a punishment brought upon humanity
by Adam's sin.

*There is a "first" death—when the soul, forsaken by
God, forsakes the body—and a "second" death—
when the soul, forsaken by God, rejoins its body for
eternal punishment.*

Having disposed of the very difficult questions concerning
the origin of our world and the beginning of the human race,
the natural order requires that we now discuss the fall of the
first man—we may say of the first men—and of the origin
and propagation of human death. For God had so made them
that, if they discharged the obligations of obedience, an angelic immortality and a blessed eternity might ensue without
the intervention of death; but if they disobeyed, death should
be visited on them with just sentence. (1)

But I see that I must speak a little more carefully of the
nature of death. For although the human soul is truly affirmed to be immortal, yet it also has a certain death of its
own. For it is called immortal, because, in a sense, it does
not cease to live and to feel; while the body is called mortal,
because it can be forsaken of all life and cannot by itself
live at all. The death, then, of the soul takes place when God
forsakes it, the death of the body when the soul forsakes it.
Therefore the death of both—that is, of the whole man—occurs when the soul, forsaken by God, forsakes the body. (2)

The first men were indeed so created that, if they had not
sinned, they would not have experienced any kind of death;
but that, having become sinners, they were so punished with
death that whatsoever sprang from their stock should also
be punished with the same death. For nothing could be born

50

of them than that which they themselves had been. Their nature deteriorated in proportion to the greatness of the condemnation of their sin, so that what existed as punishment in those who first sinned, became a natural consequence in their children. For as man the parent is, such is man the offspring; and what man was made, not when created, but when he sinned and was punished, this he propagated. (3)

And regarding what happens after death, it is no absurdity to say that death is good to the good, and evil to the evil. For the disembodied spirits of the just are at rest, but those of the wicked suffer punishment till their bodies rise again—those of the just to life everlasting, and of the others to death eternal, which is called the second death. (8)

No sooner do we begin to live in this dying body, than we begin to move ceaselessly towards death. For in the whole course of this life—if life we must call it—its mutability tends towards death. Certainly there is no one who is not closer to his death this year than last year, and to-morrow closer than to-day. For whatever time we live is deducted from our whole term of life, and that which remains is daily becoming less and less; so that our whole life is nothing but a race towards death in which no one is allowed to stand still for a little space or to go somewhat more slowly, but all are driven forward with an impartial movement and with equal rapidity. (10)

When, therefore, it is asked what death it was with which God threatened our first parents if they should transgress the commandment they had received from Him and should fail to preserve their obedience—whether it was the death of soul, or of body, or of the whole man, or that which is called second death—we must answer, It is all. For when God said to the first man, whom he had placed in Paradise, referring to the forbidden fruit, "In the day that thou eatest thereof thou shalt surely die," (Gen. 2, 17) that threatening included not only the first part of the first death, by which the soul is deprived of God; nor only the subsequent part of the first death, by which the body is deprived of the soul; nor only the whole first death itself, by which the soul is punished in separation from God and from the body, but it includes whatever of death there is, even to that final death which is called second, and to which none is subsequent. (12)

For God, the author of natures, not of vices, created man upright; but man, being of his own will corrupted, and justly condemned, begot corrupted and condemned children. For we all were in that one man, since we all were that one man who fell into sin by the woman who was made from him before the sin. To be sure, the particular forms in which we as individuals were to live had not yet been created and distributed; but already the seminal nature was there from which we were to be propagated; and since this was vitiated by sin, bound by the chain of death, and justly condemned, man could not be born of man in any other state. And thus, from the bad use of free will, there originated that whole train of evil which, with its concatenation of miseries, convoys the human race from its depraved origin, as from a corrupt root, on to the destruction of the second death, which has no end, those only being excepted who are freed by the grace of God. (14)

It may perhaps be supposed that because God said, "Ye shall die the death," and not "deaths," we should understand only that death which occurs when the soul is deserted by God, who is its life. But though we suppose that God meant only this death and that the words, "In the day ye eat of it ye shall die the death," should be understood to mean, "In the day ye desert me in disobedience, I will desert you in justice," yet assuredly in this death the other deaths also were threatened, which were its inevitable consequence. For in the first stirring of the disobedient motion which was felt in the flesh of the disobedient soul, and which caused our first parents to cover their shame, one death indeed is experienced, that, namely, which occurs when God forsakes the soul. (This was intimated by the words He uttered, when the man, stupefied by fear, had hid himself, "Adam, where are thou?" (Gen. 3, 9)—words which He used not in ignorance of inquiry, but warning him to consider where he was since God was **not** with him.) But when the soul itself forsook the body, corrupted and decayed with age, that other death was experienced of which God had spoken in pronouncing man's sentence, "Dust thou art, and unto dust shalt thou return." (Gen. 3, 19) And of these two deaths that first death of the whole man is composed. And this first death is finally followed by the second, unless man be freed by grace. (15)

BOOK XIV

On the basic difference between the earthly and
heavenly human city

*The grace of God saves some men from the kingdom
of death for the heavenly city.*

We have already stated in the preceding books that God,
who desires not only that the human race might be able, by
the similarity of nature, to associate with one another, but
also that they might be bound together in harmony and peace
by the ties of relationship, was pleased to derive all men from
one individual and created man with such a nature that the
members of this race would not have died, had not the first
two, of whom the one was created out of nothing, and the
other out of him, merited death by their disobedience; for by
them so great a sin was committed that by it the human nature was altered for the worse and was transmitted also to
their posterity liable to sin and subject to death. And the
kingdom of death so reigned over men that the deserved
penalty of sin would have hurled all headlong even unto the
second death, of which there is no end, had not the unde-
served grace of God saved some from this destiny. And thus
it has come to pass, that though there are very many and
great nations all over the earth whose rites and customs,
speech, arms, and dress are distinguished by marked differ-
ences, yet there are no more than two human societies, which
we may justly call two cities according to the language of
our Scriptures. The one city consists of those who wish to
live after the flesh, the other of those who wish to live after
the spirit; and when they severally achieve what they wish,
they live in peace, each after their kind. (1)

54

*The citizens of the city of God live according to the
spirit, i.e., according to God; the others live according
to the flesh, i.e., according to man.*

Let us see first what it is to live after the flesh and what it
is to live after the spirit. For anyone who either does not
recollect, or does not sufficiently weigh, the language of
sacred Scripture, may, on first hearing what we have said,
suppose that the Epicurean [10] philosophers live after the
flesh because they place man's highest good in bodily pleasure; and he may suppose that the Stoics,[11] who place the
supreme good of men in the soul, live after the spirit; for
what is man's soul, if not spirit? But in the sense of the
divine Scripture both are proved to live after the flesh.

For by flesh the Scripture means not only the body of a
terrestrial and mortal animal, as when it says, "All flesh is
not the same flesh, but there is one kind of flesh of men, another flesh of beasts, another of fishes, another of birds,"
(I. Cor. 15, 39) but it uses this word in many other significa-
tions; and among these various usages, a frequent one is to
use flesh for man himself, i.e., for the whole nature of man,
referring by the part to the whole, as in the words, "By the
deeds of the law there shall be no flesh justified"; (Rom. 3,
20) for what does St. Paul mean here by "no flesh" but "no
man?" And this, indeed, he shortly after says more plainly:
"No man shall be justified by the law." (Gal. 3, 11) (2)

But if anyone says that the flesh is the cause of all vices
and ill conduct inasmuch as the soul lives wickedly only because it is moved by the flesh, it is certain he has not carefully considered the whole nature of man. We believe quite
otherwise. For the corruption of the body, which weighs
down the soul, is not the cause but the punishment of the
first sin; and it was not the corruptible flesh that made the

[10] The followers of Epicurus, 341–270 B.C., son of an Athenian.
Epicurus himself set intellectual above physical pleasures, but his
disciples gradually laid the stress on sensual pleasures.
[11] Name of the followers of Zeno (ca 336–264 B.C.), who taught in
the *stoa* (hall), one of the public buildings in Athens.

soul sinful, but the sinful soul that made the flesh corruptible. And though from this corruption of the flesh there arise certain incitements to vice, and indeed vicious desires, yet we must not attribute to the flesh all the vices of a wicked life and thereby clear the devil, who has no flesh, of all sin. For it was not by having flesh, which the devil has not, but by living according to himself, that is, according to man, that man became like the devil. For the devil, too, wished to live according to himself when he did not abide in the truth. (3)

But when man lives according to himself—that is, according to man, not according to God—he assuredly lives according to a lie; not that man himself is a lie, for God, who is certainly not the author and creator of a lie, is man's author and creator, but because man was made upright that he might not live according to himself, but according to Him that made him—in other words, that he might do God's will and not his own; and not to live as he was made to live, that is a lie. For man certainly desires to be blessed even by not living so that he can be blessed. And what is a lie if this desire be not? Wherefore it is not without meaning said that all sin is a lie. For no sin is committed save by that desire or will by which we desire that it be well with us, and shrink from it being ill with us. That, therefore, is a lie which we do in order that it may be well with us, but which makes us more miserable than we were. And why is this but because the source of man's happiness lies only in God, whom he abandons when he sins, and not in himself, by living according to whom he sins?

When we said, therefore, that two diverse and conflicting human cities have arisen because some men live according to the flesh and others according to the spirit, we might equally well have said, "because some men live according to man, others according to God." (4)

The difference between living according to the flesh and according to the spirit is the difference between a good will and a bad will.

There is no need, therefore, that in our sins and vices we accuse the nature of the flesh to the injury of the Creator; for in its own nature and order the flesh is good; but to desert the Creator Good and live according to a created good is not good, whether a man choose to live according to the flesh, or according to the soul, or according to the whole human nature, which is composed of flesh and soul and which is therefore spoken of either by the name flesh alone, or by the name soul alone. For he who extols the nature of the soul as the chief good and condemns the nature of the flesh as if it were evil, assuredly is fleshly both in his love of the soul and in his hatred of the flesh; for his feelings arise from human fancy, not from divine truth. (5)

What is important, however, is the character of the human will. Because if the will is wrong, the motions of the soul (such as desire, fear, joy and sorrow) will be wrong, but if the will is right, they will be not merely blameless but praiseworthy. For the will is in all these motions; indeed, none of them is anything else but will. For what are desire and joy but a volition of consent to the things we wish? And what are fear and sadness but a volition of aversion from the things which we do not wish? When consent takes the form of seeking to possess the things we wish, we speak of desire; and when consent takes the form of enjoying the things we wish, we speak of joy. In like manner, when we turn with aversion from that which we do not wish to happen, this volition is termed fear; and when we turn away from that which has happened against our will, this act of will is called sorrow. Wherefore the man who lives according to God, and not according to man, ought to be a lover of good, and therefore a hater of evil. (6)

The right will, in other words, is well-directed love, and the wrong will is ill-directed love. But love yearning to have what is loved, is desire; love having and enjoying what is loved, is joy; love fleeing what is opposed to it, is fear; and love feeling what is opposed to it when it has befallen it, is sadness. Now all these four motions are evil if the love is evil; and they are good if the love is good. (7)

The citizens of the holy city of God, who live according to God in the pilgrimage of this life, both fear and desire, and grieve and rejoice. And because their love is rightly placed, all these affections of theirs are right. They fear eternal punishment, they desire eternal life; they grieve because they themselves groan within themselves, waiting for the adoption, the redemption of their body; they rejoice in hope, because there "shall be brought to pass the saying that is written: 'Death is swallowed up in victory.' " (I. Cor. 15, 54) In like manner they fear to sin, they desire to persevere; they grieve in sin, they rejoice in good works. They fear to sin because they hear that, "because iniquity shall abound, the love of many shall wax cold." (Matt. 24, 12) They desire to persevere because they hear that it is written, "He that endureth to the end shall be saved." (Matt. 10, 22)

Since these affections, when they are exercised in a becoming way, follow the guidance of right reason, who will dare to say that they are diseases or vicious passions? Wherefore even the Lord Himself, when He condescended to lead a human life in the form of a slave, but without any sin whatever, exercised these emotions where He judged they should be exercised. For as there was in Him a true human body and a true human soul, so was there also a true human emotion. When, therefore, we read in the Gospel that, when about to raise Lazarus, He even shed tears, that He earnestly desired to eat the passover with His disciples, that, as His passion drew near, His soul was sorrowful, these emotions are certainly not falsely ascribed to Him.

In the blessed life eternal there will be love and joy, not only right, but also assured; but fear and grief there will be none. Whence it already appears in some sort what manner of persons the citizens of the city of God must be in this their pilgrimage, who live after the spirit, not after the flesh— that is to say, according to God, not according to man—and also what manner of persons they shall be in that immortality whither they are journeying. But the city or society of the wicked, who live not according to God, but according to man, is shaken by those wicked emotions as by diseases and disturbances. And if there be some of its citizens who seem to restrain and, as it were, temper these passions, they are so elated with ungodly pride that their disease is as much greater as their pain is less. And if some, with a vanity monstrous in proportion to its rarity, have become enamoured of themselves because they can no longer be stimulated and excited by any emotion, moved or bent by no affection, such persons rather lose all humanity than obtain true tranquillity. For a thing is not necessarily right because it is inflexible, nor healthy because it is insensible. (9)

And again—as was the case with the wicked angels—
a good will becomes evil by spontaneously turning
away from a higher good to a lower good.

But because God foresaw all things and was therefore not ignorant that man also would fall, we ought to consider this holy city in connection with what God foresaw and ordained, and not according to our own ideas, which do not embrace God's ordination. For man, by his sin, could not disturb the divine counsel, nor compel God to change what He had decreed; for God's foreknowledge had anticipated both—that is to say, both how evil the man whom He had created good should become, and for what good He Himself should even thus use him. God, as it is written, made man upright, and therefore with a good will. For if man had not had a good will, he could not have been upright. The good will, then, is the work of God; for God created him with it. But the first evil will, which preceded all man's evil acts, was a kind of falling away from the work of God to its own works rather than any positive work. (11)

This falling away is spontaneous; for if the will had remained steadfast in the love of that higher and changeless good which had enlightened the will to understand and to love the good, it would not have turned away to find satisfaction in itself, and so become blind and cold; the woman would not have believed the serpent spoke the truth, nor would the man have preferred the request of his wife to the command of God. The wicked deed, then—that is to say, the transgression of eating the forbidden fruit—was committed by persons who were already wicked. But man did not so fall away as to become absolutely nothing; but, being turned towards himself, his being became more contracted than it was when he clave to Him who supremely is. Accordingly, to exist in himself, that is, to be his own satisfaction after abandoning God, is not quite to become a nonentity but to approximate to that. It is good to have the heart lifted up, yet not to one's self, for this is proud, but to the Lord, for this is obedient and can be the act only of the humble. And therefore humility, by making us subject to God, exalts us. But pride, being a defect of nature, by the very act of refusing subjection and revolting from Him who is supreme, falls to a low condition. And therefore humility is specially recommended to the city of God as it sojourns in this world, and is specially exhibited in the city of God and in the person of Christ its King; while the contrary vice of pride, according to the testimony of the sacred writings, specially rules his adversary the devil.

And certainly this is the great difference which distinguishes the two cities of which we speak, the one being the society of the godly men, the other the ungodly, each associated with the angels that adhere to their party, and the one guided and fashioned by love of self, the other by love of God. The devil, then, would not have ensnared man in the open and manifest sin of doing what God had forbidden, had man not already begun to live for himself. It was this that made him listen with pleasure to the words, "Ye shall be as gods," (Gen. 3, 5) which they would much more readily have accomplished by obediently adhering to their supreme and true end than by proudly living to themselves. For created gods are gods not by virtue of what is in themselves, but by a participation of the true God. By craving to be more, man becomes less; and by aspiring to be self-sufficing, he fell away from Him who truly suffices him. (13)

In short, to say all in a word, what but disobedience was the punishment of disobedience in that sin? For what else is man's misery but his own disobedience to himself, so that in consequence of his not being willing to do what he could do, he now wills to do what he cannot. For though he could do all things in Paradise before he sinned, yet he wished to do only what he could do, and therefore he could do all the things he wished. (15)

And yet we long for blessedness, knowing that true blessedness must be eternal.

However, if we look at this a little more closely, we see that no one lives as he wishes but the blessed, and that no one is blessed but the righteous. But even the righteous himself does not live as he wishes until he has arrived where he cannot die, be deceived, or injured, and until he is assured that this shall be his eternal condition. For this human nature demands; and nature is not fully and perfectly blessed till it attains what it seeks. But what man is at present able to live as he wishes, when it is not even in his power to live? He wishes to live, he is compelled to die. How, then, does he live as he wishes who does not live as long as he wishes? Or if he wishes to die, how can he live as he wishes, since he does not wish even to live? Or if he wishes to die, not because he dislikes life, but that after death he may live better, still he is not yet living as he wishes, but only has the prospect of so living when, through death, he reaches that which he wishes. But admit that he lives as he wishes because he has done violence to himself and forced himself not to wish what he cannot obtain, and to wish only what he can, is he therefore blessed because he is patiently wretched? For a blessed life is possessed only by the man who loves it. If it is loved and possessed, it must necessarily be more ardently loved than all

besides; for whatever else is loved must be loved for the sake
of the blessed life. And if it is loved as it deserves to be—
and the man is not blessed who does not love the blessed life
as it deserves—then he who so loves it cannot but wish it to
be eternal. Therefore it shall then only be blessed when it is
eternal. (25)

*Man could not have remained upright without divine
help—i.e., without acknowledging that he was merely
a creature.*

Man had been so constituted that, if he looked to God for
help, man's goodness should defeat the angel's wickedness;
but if by proud self-pleasing he abandoned God, his Creator
and Sustainer, he should be conquered. If his will remained
upright, through leaning on God's help, he should be rewarded; if it became wicked, by forsaking God, he should
be punished. But even this trusting in God's help could not
itself be accomplished without God's help, although man had
it in his own power to relinquish the benefits of divine grace
by pleasing himself. For as it is not in our power to live in
this world without sustaining ourselves by food, while it is
in our power to refuse this nourishment and cease to live, as
those do who kill themselves, so it was not in man's power,
even in Paradise, to live as he ought without God's help; but
it was in his power to live wickedly, though thus he should
cut short his happiness and incur very just punishment. Since,
then, God was not ignorant that man would fall, why should
He not have suffered him to be tempted by an angel who
hated and envied him? It was not, indeed, that He was un-
aware that he should be conquered, but because He foresaw
that by man's seed, aided by divine grace, this same devil
himself should be conquered, to the greater glory of the
saints. Without any future event escaping God's foreknowledge, and without his foreknowledge compelling anyone to
sin, all this was brought about so as to demonstrate in the
experience of the intelligent creation, human and angelic,

how great a difference there is between the private presumption of the creature and the Creator's protection. For who will dare to believe or say that it was not in God's power to prevent both angels and men from sinning? But God preferred to leave this in their power and thus to show both what evil could be wrought by their pride, and what good by His grace. (27)

The difference between the two cities rests on the difference between love of self and love of God.

Accordingly, two cities have been formed by two loves: the earthly by the love of self, even to the contempt of God; the heavenly by the love of God, even to the contempt of self. The former, in a word, glories in itself, the latter in the Lord. For the one seeks glory from men; but the greatest glory of the other is God. The one lifts up its head in its own glory; the other says to its God, "Thou art my glory, and the lifter up of mine head." (Ps. 3, 3) In the one, the princes and the nations it subdues are ruled by the love of ruling; in the other, the princes and the subjects serve one another in love, the latter obeying, while the former take thought for all. The one delights in its own strength, represented in the persons of its rulers; the other says to its God, "I will love Thee, O Lord, my strength." (Ps. 18, 1) (28)

BOOK XV

The history of the two cities from Adam to Noah

Cain, Adam's first-born son and the first city builder, belonged to the city of men. Abel, who was born after Cain, belonged to the city of God.

Of the bliss of Paradise, of Paradise itself, of the life of our first parents there, and of their sin and punishment, many have thought much, spoken much, written much. We ourselves, too, have spoken of these things in the foregoing books and have written either what we read in the Holy Scriptures or what we could reasonably deduce from them. And were we to enter into a more detailed investigation of these matters, an endless number of endless questions would arise which would involve us in a larger work than the present occasion admits. We cannot be expected to find room for replying to every question that may be started by unoccupied and captious men who are ever more ready to ask questions than capable of understanding the answer. Yet I trust we have already done justice to these great and difficult questions regarding the beginning of the world, or of the soul, or of the human race itself. This race we have divided into two parts, the one consisting of those who live according to man, the other of those who live according to God. And these we also call the two cities, or the two communities of men, of which the one is predestined to reign eternally with God, and the other to suffer eternal punishment with the devil. This, however, is their end, and of it we speak afterwards.

At present, as we have said enough about their origin, whether among the angels, whose numbers we know not, or in the two first human beings, it seems suitable to attempt an account of their career from the time when our two first parents began to propagate the race until all human generation shall cease. For this whole time or world-age in which the dying exit and those who are born succeed is the career of the two cities with which we deal. Of these two first parents of the human race, then, Cain was the first-born, and he belonged to the city of men; after him was born Abel, who belonged to the city of God. For what is true for every individual—concerning which the apostle stated, "that is not first which is spiritual, but that which is natural, and afterward that which is spiritual," (I. Cor. 15, 46) whence it comes to pass that each man, being derived from a condemned stock, is first of all born of Adam evil and carnal and becomes good and spiritual only afterwards when he is grafted into Christ by regeneration—so was it in the human race as a whole: when these two cities began to run their course by a series of deaths and births, the citizen of this world was born first, and after him was born the pilgrim in this world, the citizen of the city of God, predestined by grace, elected by grace, by grace a pilgrim below, and by grace a citizen above.

By grace, for so far as regards himself he had come from the same mass which had been condemned in its entirety at the beginning; but God, like a potter—this comparison is introduced by the apostle judiciously, and not without thought —made of the same lump one vessel to honour, another to dishonour. But first the vessel to dishonour was made, and after it another to honour. For in each individual, as I have already said, there is first of all that which is wicked and disapproved, that from which we must begin, but in which we need not necessarily remain; afterwards is that which is well-approved, to which we may by advancing attain, and in which, when we have reached it, we may abide. Not, indeed, that every wicked man shall be good, but that no one will be good who was not first of all wicked. Accordingly, it is recorded of Cain that he built a city, but Abel, being a sojourner, built none. For the city of the saints is above, although here below it begets citizens in whom it lives as a pilgrim until the time of its reign arrives, when it shall gather together all its citizens in the day of the resurrection of the body; and then shall the promised kingdom be given to them in which they shall reign with their Prince, the King of the Ages, time without end. (1)

The earthly city, which shall not be everlasting—for it will no longer be a city when it has been committed to the extreme penalty—has its good in this world, and it rejoices in it with such joy as such things can afford. But as this is not a good which can free its lovers of all difficulties, this city is often divided against itself by litigations, wars, quarrels, and such victories as are either life-destroying or short-lived. For each part of this city which fights against another part seeks to triumph over the nations, though it is itself in bondage to vice.

Nevertheless, the things which this city desires cannot justly be said to be evil, for it is itself, in its own kind, better than all other human good. For it desires earthly peace for the sake of enjoying earthly goods. This peace is purchased by toilsome wars; and it is obtained by what they call a glorious victory. Now, when victory remains with the party which had the juster cause, who hesitates to congratulate the victor and to term it a desirable peace? These things, then, are good things and without doubt the gifts of God. But if they neglect the better things of the heavenly city, which are secured by eternal victory and peace never-ending, and covet these present good things so inordinately that they believe them to be the only desirable things, loving them even better than those things which are believed to be better, then it is necessary that misery follow and ever increase. (4)

Cain, the founder of the earthly city, slew his brother Abel, just as Romulus, the founder of Rome, slew his brother Remus.

The founder of the earthly city was a fratricide. Overcome with envy, he slew his own brother, a citizen of the eternal city and a pilgrim on earth. So we cannot be surprised that this archetype of crime should, long afterwards, be repeated at the foundation of that city which was destined to reign over so many nations and to be the head of this earthly city of which we speak. For of Rome also, as one of their poets has mentioned, "the first walls were stained with a brother's blood," or, as Roman history records, Remus was slain by his brother Romulus. And thus there is no difference between the foundation of Rome and that of the earthly city, unless it be that Romulus and Remus were both citizens of the earthly city. Both Romulus and Remus desired to have the glory of founding the Roman republic, but both could not have as much glory as if only one claimed it; for he who wished to have the glory of ruling would certainly rule less if his power were shared by a living consort. In order, therefore, that the whole glory might be enjoyed by one, his consort was removed; and by this crime the empire was made, indeed, larger, but also inferior, while otherwise it would have been less but better.

Now these brothers, Cain and Abel, were not both animated by the same earthly desires, nor did the murderer envy the other because he feared that, by both ruling, his own dominion would be curtailed, for Abel was not anxious to rule in that city which his brother built. Cain was moved by that diabolical, envious hatred with which the evil regard the good just because the good are good while they themselves are evil. For the possession of goodness is by no means diminished by being shared with a permanent or temporary partner; on the contrary, the possession of goodness is increased in proportion to the concord and charity of each of those who share it. In short, he who is unwilling to share this possession cannot have it; and he who is most willing to admit others to a share of it will have the greatest abundance to himself. The quarrel, then, between Romulus and Remus shows how the earthly city is divided against itself; the quarrel between Cain and Abel illustrates the hatred that subsists between the two cities, between that of God and that of men. The wicked war with the wicked; the good also war with the wicked. But with the good, good men, or at least perfectly good men, cannot war. (5)

And therefore it is said to the good who are growing in grace and living in this pilgrimage by faith, "Bear ye one another's burdens, and so fulfil the law of Christ. (Gal. 6, 2) (6)

Cain's act was entirely voluntary: he could have controlled his envy.

Though God spoke to Cain in that manner by which He was wont to accommodate Himself to our first parents when he conversed with them, by assuming the form of his own creature, as a companion, what good influence had it on Cain? Did he not fulfil his wicked intention of killing his brother even after he was warned by God's voice? For when God had made a distinction between their sacrifices, rejecting Cain's, accepting Abel's, a distinction which was doubtless intimated by some visible sign; and when God had done so because the works of the one were evil and those of his brother good, Cain was very wroth and his countenance fell. This angry regret for another person's goodness, even his brother's, was held against him by God as a great sin. And He accused him of it with the interrogation, "Why art thou wroth, and why is thy countenance fallen?" (Gen. 4, 6) For God saw that he envied his brother, and of this He accused him.

Yet God does not dismiss Cain without counsel, holy, just, and good. "Fret not thyself," He says, "for unto thee shall be his turning, and thou shalt rule over him." (Gen. 4, 7) Over his brother, does He mean? Most certainly not. Over what, then, but sin? For He had said, "Thou hast sinned," and then He added, "Fret not thyself, for to thee shall be *its* turning, and thou shalt rule over *it*." [12] If we understand this sin to be that carnal concupiscence of which the apostle says, "The flesh lusteth against the spirit," (Gal. 5, 17) among the fruits

[12] The Latin *conversio eius* can be rendered either by "his turning" or by "its turning."

of which lust he names envy, by which assuredly Cain was stung and excited to destroy his brother, then we may properly read, "To thee shall be *its* turning, and thou shalt rule over *it*." For when the carnal part of us—that part which the apostle calls sin in that passage where he says, "It is not I who do it, but sin that dwelleth in me," (Rom. 7, 17) the part which the philosophers call vicious, the part which ought not to lead the mind, but which the mind ought to rule and restrain by reason from illicit motions—when this part is straining to perpetrate any wickedness, it is turned once it is curbed towards the mind and subdued and conquered by it, so that reason rules over it as a subject. It was this which God enjoined on him who was kindled with the fire of envy against his brother, so that he sought to put out of the way him whom he should have set as an example. "Fret not thyself," or compose thyself, God says: withhold thy hand from crime; let not sin reign in your mortal body to effect what it desires, nor let your members be instruments of unrighteousness unto sin. "For to thee shall be its turning," so long as you do not encourage sin by giving it the rein, but bridle it by quenching its fire. "And thou shalt rule over it"; for when it is not allowed any external actings it yields itself to the rule of the governing mind and righteous will. But Cain received that counsel of God in the spirit of one who did not wish to amend. In fact, the vice of envy grew stronger in him; and, having entrapped his brother, he slew him. Such was the founder of the earthly city. (7)

Cain founded the first civic community, i.e., a multitude of men bound together by some associating tie.

But now I must come to the defense of sacred history, so that Scripture may not be reckoned incredible when it relates that one man built a city at a time in which there seem to have been but four men upon earth, or rather indeed but three after one brother slew the other—namely the first man,

Adam, the father of all, Cain himself, and his son Enoch, by
whose name the city was called.

But they who are moved by this consideration forget to
take into account that the writer of the sacred history does
not necessarily mention all the men who might be alive at
that time but those only whom the scope of his work required
him to name. The design of that writer—who in this matter
was the instrument of the Holy Ghost—was to descend to
Abraham through the successions of ascertained generations
propagated from one man and then to pass from Abraham's
seed to the people of God, in whom, separated as they were
from other nations, was prefigured and predicted all that relates to that city whose reign is eternal, and to its king and
founder Christ, which things were foreseen in the Spirit as
destined to come. However, this objective is not accomplished without saying anything of the other society of men
which we call the earthly city, but mention is made of it so
far as seemed needful to enhance the glory of the heavenly
city by contrast to its opposite.

Accordingly, when the divine Scripture, in mentioning the
number of years which those men lived, concludes its account
of each man of whom it speaks with the words, "And he
begat sons and daughters, and all his days were so and so,
and he died," are we to understand that, because it does not
name those sons and daughters, therefore, during that long
term of years over which one lifetime extended in those early
days, there might not have been born very many men by
whose united numbers not one but several cities might have
been built?

It suited the purpose of God, by whose inspiration these
histories were composed, to arrange and distinguish from the
first these two societies in their several generations—that on
the one side the generations of men, i.e., of those who live
according to man, and on the other side the generations of
the sons of God, i.e., of men living according to God, might
be traced down together and yet apart from one another as
far as the deluge, at which point their dissociation and asso-

ciation are exhibited: their dissociation, inasmuch as the generations of both lines are recorded in separate tables, the one
line descending from the fratricide Cain, the other from
Seth, who had been born to Adam instead of him whom his
brother slew; their association, inasmuch as the good so deteriorated that the whole race became of such a character
that it was swept away by the deluge with the exception of
one just man, whose name was Noah, and his wife and three
sons and three daughters-in-law, which eight persons were
alone deemed worthy to escape from that desolating visita-
tion which destroyed all men. Therefore, although it is written, "And Cain knew his wife, and she conceived and bare
Enoch, and he builded a city and called the name of the city
after the name of his son Enoch," (Gen. 4, 17) it does not
follow that we are to believe this to have been his first-born;
for we cannot suppose that this is proved by the expression
"he knew his wife," as if then for the first time he had had
intercourse with her. For in the case of Adam, the father of
all, this expression is used not only when Cain, who seems to
have been his first-born, was conceived, but also afterwards,
when the same Scripture says, "Adam knew his wife again
and she conceived and bare a son, and called his name Seth."
(Gen. 4, 25) Whence it is obvious that Scripture employs
this expression neither always when a birth is recorded nor
then only when the birth of a first-born is mentioned. Neither
is it necessary to suppose that Enoch was Cain's first-born
because he named his city after him. For it is quite possible
that though he had other sons, yet for some reason his father
loved him more than the rest. But even though Enoch was
the first-born of the city's founder, that is no reason for supposing that the father named the city after him as soon as he
was born; for at that time he, being but a solitary man, could
not have founded a civic community, which is nothing else
than a multitude of men bound together by some associating
tie. But when his family increased to such numbers that he
had quite a population, then it became possible to him both
to build a city and to give it, when founded, the name of his

son. For so long was the life of those antediluvians that he who lived the shortest time of those whose years are mentioned in Scripture attained to the age of 753 years. (8)

Let us now see how it can be plainly made out that in the enormously protracted lives of those men the years were not so short that ten of their years were equal to only one of ours, but were of as great length as our own, which are measured by the course of the sun. Scripture states that the flood occurred in the six hundredth year of Noah's life. But why is it also written, in the same place "The waters of the flood were upon the earth in the six hundredth year of Noah's life, in the second month, the twenty-seventh day of the month," (Gen. 7, 10) if that very brief year of which it took ten to make one of ours consisted of thirty-six days? For so scant a year, if the ancient usage dignified it with the name of year, either has not months, or its month must be three days, so that it may have twelve of them.

It is plain that the day then was what it is now: a period of four-and-twenty hours, determined by the lapse of day and night; the month then equal to the month now: defined by the rise and completion of one moon; the year then equal to the year now: completed by twelve lunar months, with the addition of five days and a-fourth to adjust it with the course of the sun. It was a year of this length which was reckoned the six hundredth of Noah's life; and in the second month, the twenty-seventh day of the month, the flood began. (14)

The Scriptures record two series of generations between Adam and the deluge, but in the line which represents the city of God there was not only generation but also regeneration.

That which is undeniable is that Cain was the first who was born of man and woman. For had he not been the first who was added by birth to the two unborn persons, Adam could not have said what he is recorded to have said, "I have gotten a man by the Lord." (Gen. 4, 1) He was followed by

Abel, whom the elder brother slew, and who was the first to show, by a kind of foreshadowing of the sojourning city of God, what iniquitous persecutions that city would suffer at the hands of wicked and, as it were, earth-born men, who love their earthly origin and delight in the earthly happiness of the earthly city. But how old Adam was when he begat these sons does not appear. After this the generations diverge, the one branch deriving from Cain, the other from him whom Adam begot in the stead of Abel slain by his brother and whom he called Seth, saying, as it is written, "For God hath raised me up another seed for Abel whom Cain slew." (Gen. 4, 25)

These two series of generations, the one of Cain, the other of Seth, represent the two cities in their distinctive ranks, the one the heavenly city, which sojourns on earth, the other the earthly, which gapes after earthly joys and grovels in them as if they were the only joys.

But though eight generations, including Adam, are registered before the flood, no man of Cain's line has his age recorded at which the son who succeeded him was begotten. For the Spirit of God refused to mark the times before the flood in the generations of the earthly city, but preferred to do so in the heavenly line, as if it were more worthy of being remembered. (15)

As the human race, subsequently to the first marriage of the man who was made of dust and his wife who was made out of his side, required the union of males and females in order that it might multiply, and as there were no human beings except those who had been born of these two, men took their sisters for wives—an act which was as certainly dictated by necessity in these ancient days as afterwards it was condemned by the prohibitions of religion.

The sexual intercourse of man and woman, then, is in the case of mortals a kind of seed-bed of the city; but while the earthly city needs for its population only generation, the heavenly needs also regeneration to rid it of the taint of generation. Whether before the deluge there was any bodily or visible sign of regeneration, such as was afterwards enjoined upon Abraham when he was circumcised, or what kind of sign it was, the sacred history does not inform us. (16)

Only Noah and his family survived the deluge which ended this first period of human history. The ark itself is not merely a historical fact but a symbol of the church.

When the human race increased and advanced, there arose a mixture and confusion of the two cities by their participation in a common iniquity.[13] And this calamity, as well as the first, was occasioned by woman, although not in the same way; for these women did not persuade the men to sin, but having belonged to the earthly city and to the society of the earthly, they had been of corrupt manners from the first, and they were loved for their bodily beauty by the sons of God, i.e., by the citizens of the other city which merely sojourns in this world. Beauty is indeed a good gift of God; but that the good may not think it a great good, God dispenses it even to the wicked. And thus, when the good that is great and proper to the good was abandoned by the sons of God, they fell to a paltry good which is not peculiar to the good, but common to the good and the evil; and when they were captivated by the daughters of men, they adopted the manners of the earthly to win them as their brides, and they forsook the godly ways they had followed in their own holy society. And thus beauty, which is indeed God's handiwork, but only a temporal, carnal, and lower kind of good, is not fitly loved in preference to God, the eternal, spiritual, and unchangeable good. When the miser prefers his gold to justice, it is through no fault of the gold, but of the man; and so with every created thing. For though it be good, it may be loved with an evil as well as with a good love: it is loved

[13] Augustine refers to the passage, Gen. 6, 1–2: "And it came to pass . . . that the sons of God saw the daughters of men that they were fair; and they took them wives of all which they chose."

rightly when it is loved ordinately; evilly, when inordinately.

It seems to me that it is a brief but true definition of virtue to say that it is ordered love; and on this account, in the Canticles, the bride of Christ, the city of God, sings, "He has ordered love within me." (Cant. 2, 4) It was the order of this love, then, which the sons of God disturbed when they forsook God and were enamoured of the daughters of men. And by these two names—sons of God and daughters of men—the two cities are sufficiently distinguished. For though the former were by nature children of men, they had come into possession of another name by grace. (22)

"The Lord God saw that the wickedness of man was great in the earth, and that every imagination of the thoughts of his heart was only evil continually. And it repented the Lord that he had made man on the earth, and it grieved Him at His heart. And the Lord said, 'I will destroy man, whom I have created, from the face of the earth; both man and beast, and the creeping thing, and the fowls of the air: for I am angry that I have made them.' " (Gen. 6, 5–7) (24)

The anger of God is not a disturbing emotion of His mind, but a judgment by which punishment is inflicted upon sin. He does not, like man, repent of anything He has done, because in all matters His decision is as inflexible as His prescience is certain. But if Scripture were not to use such expressions as the above, it would not familiarly insinuate itself into the minds of all classes of men, whom it seeks access to for their good, that it may alarm the proud, arouse the careless, exercise the inquisitive, and satisfy the intelligent; and this it could not do, did it not first stoop and, in a manner, descend to them. (25)

Moreover, inasmuch as God commanded Noah, a just man, and, as the truthful Scripture says, a man perfect in his generation—perfect not indeed with the perfection of the citizens of the city of God in that immortal condition in which they equal the angels, but perfect in so far as they can be perfect in their sojourn in this world—inasmuch as God commanded him, I say, to make an ark in which he might be rescued from the destruction of the flood along with his family, i.e., his wife, sons, and daughters-in-law, and along with the animals who, in obedience to God's command, came to him in the ark: this is certainly a figure of the city of God, which sojourns in this wicked world as in a deluge.

Now anyone may object to this interpretation and may give another which harmonizes with the rule of faith. (26) Yet no one ought to suppose either that these things were written for no purpose, or that we should study only the historical truth, apart from the allegorical meanings; or, on the contrary, that they are only allegories, and that there were no such facts at all, or that, whether it be so or no, there is here no prophecy of the church. For what right-minded man will contend that books so religiously preserved during thousands of years, and transmitted by so orderly a succession, were written without an object, or that only the bare historical facts are to be considered when we read them?

And since this is so, if not even the most audacious will presume to assert that these things were written without a purpose, or that, although the events really happened, they have no symbolical meaning, or that they did not really happen, but are only allegory, or that at all events they are far from having any figurative reference to the church; if it has been made out that, on the other hand, we must rather believe that there was a wise purpose in committing these events to memory and to writing, that they did happen, and they do have a symbolical meaning, and that this significance has a prophetic reference to the church, then this book, having served its purpose, may now be closed, so that we may go on to trace in the history subsequent to the deluge the courses of the two cities—the earthly, that lives according to men, and the heavenly, that lives according to God. (27)

BOOK XVI

The history of the two cities from Noah to
Abraham; the history of the heavenly city from
Abraham to David

*Though, between Noah and Abraham, no righteous
individual is mentioned by Scripture, we can assume
that the city of God continued to exist.*

It is difficult to discover from Scripture whether, after the
deluge, traces of the holy city are continuous, or whether
they are so interrupted by intervening seasons of godlessness
that not a single worshipper of the one true God was found
among men; because from Noah, who, with his wife, three
sons, and as many daughters-in-law, achieved deliverance in
the ark from the destruction of the deluge, down to Abraham, we do not find in the canonical books that the piety of
anyone is celebrated by express divine testimony, unless it
be in the case of Noah, who commands with a prophetic
benediction his two sons Shem and Japheth while he beheld
and foresaw what was long afterwards to happen. (1)

From the blessing of the two sons of Noah and the cursing
of the middle son, there is, as I have said, down to Abraham,
i.e., for more than a thousand years, no mention of any
righteous persons who worshipped God. I do not therefore
conclude that there were none; but it would have been tedious to mention everyone, and would have displayed historical accuracy rather than prophetic foresight. The object
of the writer of these sacred books, or rather of the spirit of
God in him, is not only to record the past, but to depict the
future so far as it regards the city of God. (2)

The tower of Babel and the confusion of tongues.

The total number of the progeny of the three sons of Noah is seventy-three, fifteen by Japheth, thirty-one by Ham, twenty-seven by Shem. Then Scripture adds, "These are the sons of Shem, after their families, after their tongues, in their lands, after their nations." (Gen. 10, 31) And so of the whole number: "These are the families of the sons of Noah after their generations, in their nations; and by means of these were the nations dispersed over the earth after the flood." (Gen. 10, 32) From which we gather that the seventy-three—or rather, as I shall presently show, seventy-two—were not individuals but nations (3)

But though these nations are said to have been dispersed according to their languages, yet the narrator recurs to that time when all had but one language and explains how it came to pass that a diversity of languages was introduced. "The whole earth," he says, "was of one language, and of one speech. And it came to pass, as they journeyed from the east, that they found a plain in the land of Shinar, and they dwelt there. And they said one to another, 'Come and let us make bricks, and burn them thoroughly.' And they had bricks for stone, and slime had they for mortar. And they said, 'Come, and let us build us a city and a tower whose top shall reach unto heaven; and let us make us a name, lest we be scattered abroad on the face of the whole earth.' And the Lord came down to see the city and the tower which the children of men builded. And the Lord said, 'Behold, the people is one, and they have all one language; and this they begin to do: and now nothing will be restrained from them, which they have imagined to do. Come, and let us go down and confound there their language, that they may not understand one another's speech.' And God scattered them abroad from thence upon the face of all the earth: and they left off to build the city. Therefore is the name of it called Babel, i.e., Confusion; because the Lord did there confound the language of all the earth: and from thence did the Lord scatter them abroad upon the face of all the earth." (Gen. 11, 1–9) This city, which was called Confusion, is the same as Babylon, whose wonderful construction Gentile history also notices. The giant Nimrod was its founder, as had been hinted a little before, where Scripture, in speaking of him, says that the beginning of his kingdom was Babylon, that is, Babylon had a supremacy over the other cities as the metropolis and royal residence; although it did not rise to the grand dimensions designed by its proud and impious founder. He and his people, therefore, erected this tower against the Lord and so gave expression to their impious pride; and justly was their wicked intention punished by God, even though it was unsuccessful. But what was the nature of the punishment? As the tongue is the instrument of domination, in it pride was punished; so that man, who would not understand God when He issued His commands, should be misunderstood when he himself gave orders. Thus was that conspiracy disbanded, for each man retired from those he could not understand and associated with those whose speech was intelligible; and the nations were divided according to their languages and scattered over the earth as seemed good to God, who accomplished this in ways hidden from and incomprehensible to us. (4)

From the three sons of Noah, therefore, 73, or rather, as the catalogue will show, 72 nations and as many languages were dispersed over the earth, and as they increased filled even the islands. But the nations multiplied much more than the language; and who can doubt that, as the human race increased, men contrived to pass to the islands in ships? (6)

But as to the fable that there are Antipodes, that is to say, men on the opposite side of the earth, where the sun rises when it sets to us, men who walk with their feet opposite ours, that is on no ground credible. And, indeed, it is not affirmed that this has been learned by historical knowledge, but by scientific conjecture on the ground that the earth is suspended within the concavity of the sky and that it has as much room on the one side of it as on the other: hence they say that the part which is beneath must also be inhabited. But they do not remark that, although it be supposed or scientifically demonstrated that the world is of a round and spherical form, yet it does not follow that the other side of the earth is bare of water; nor even, though it be bare, does it immediately follow that it is peopled. For Scripture, which proves the truth of its historical statements by the accomplishment of its prophecies, gives no false information; and it is too absurd to say that some men might have taken ship, traversed the whole wide ocean and crossed from this side of the world to the other, and that thus even the inhabitants of that distant region are descended from that one first man. Wherefore let us seek if we can find the city of God that sojourns on earth among these human races who are catalogued as having been divided into seventy-two nations and as many languages. For it continued down to the deluge and the ark and is proved to have existed still among the sons of Noah by their blessings, and chiefly in the eldest son Shem. (9)

The original language of Adam, i.e., Hebrew, was preserved in the genealogical line that leads to Abraham.

Scripture, after exhibiting the earthly city as Babylon or "Confusion," reverts to the patriarch Shem, and omitting the other sons of Shem, who are not concerned in this matter, Scripture gives the genealogy to those by whom the line runs on to Abraham, as before the flood those are given who carried on the line to Noah from Seth. Accordingly this series of generations begins thus: "These are the generations of Shem: Shem was an hundred years old, and begat Arphaxad two years after the flood. And Shem lived after he begat Arphaxad five hundred years, and begat sons and daughters." In like manner it registers the rest, naming the year of his life in which each begat the son who belonged to that line which extends to Abraham. There are thus from the flood to Abraham 1072 years.

When, therefore, we look for the city of God in these

seventy-two nations, we cannot affirm that while they had but one lip, that is, one language, the human race had departed from the worship of the true God, and that genuine godliness had survived only in those generations which descend from Shem through Arphaxad and reach to Abraham; but from the time they proudly built a tower to heaven, a symbol of godless exaltation, the city or society of the wicked becomes apparent. Whether it was only disguised before, or non-existent; whether both cities remained after the flood—the godly in the two sons of Noah who were blessed, and in their posterity, and the ungodly in the cursed son and his descendants, from whom sprang that mighty hunter against the Lord—is not easily determined. (10)

As the fact of all using one language did not secure the absence of sin-infected men from the race—for even before the deluge there was one language, and yet all but the single family of just Noah were found worthy of destruction by the flood—so when the nations, by a prouder godlessness, earned the punishment of the dispersion and of the confusion of tongues, and the city of the godless was called Confusion or Babylon, there was still the house of Heber in which the primitive language of the race survived. Because when the other races were divided by their own peculiar languages, Heber's family preserved that language which is not unreasonably believed to have been the common language of the race. It was thenceforth named Hebrew. We are induced to believe that this was the primitive and common language because the multiplication and change of languages was introduced as a punishment, and it is fit to ascribe to the people of God an immunity from this punishment. Nor is it without significance that this is the language which Abraham retained and which he could not transmit to all his descendants, but only to those of Jacob's line, who distinctively and eminently constituted God's people, received His covenants, and were Christ's progenitors according to the flesh. In the same way, Heber himself did not transmit that language to all his

posterity, but only to the line from which Abraham sprang.
(11)

Let us now survey the progress of the city of God from the
era of the patriarch Abraham, from whose time the city itself
begins to be more conspicuous and the divine promises,
which are now fulfilled in Christ, begin to be more fully revealed. We learn, then, from the intimations of holy Scripture, that Abraham was born in the country of the Chaldeans,
a land belonging to the Assyrian Empire. Now, even at that
time impious superstitions were rife with the Chaldeans, as
with other nations. The family of Terah, to which Abraham
belonged, was the only one in which the worship of the true
God survived, and the only one, we may suppose, in which
the Hebrew language was preserved. (12)

*Abraham is promised that he will be the spiritual
father of the city of God.*

Next it is related how Terah with his family left the region
of the Chaldeans and came into Mesopotamia, and dwelt in
Haran. The narrative runs thus: "And Terah took Abram
his son, and Lot the son of Haran, his son's son, and Sarah
his daughter-in-law, his son Abram's wife, and they went
forth with them from Ur of the Chaldees, to go into the land
of Canaan; and they came unto Haran, and dwelt there."
(Gen. 11, 31) (13)

"Now the Lord had said unto Abram, 'Get thee out of thy
country, and from thy kindred, and from thy father's house,
unto a land that I will show thee: and I will make of thee a
great nation, and I will bless thee, and make thy name great:
and thou shalt be a blessing and I will bless them that bless
thee, and curse them that curse thee: and in thee shall all
tribes of the earth be blessed.' " (Gen. 12, 1–2) Now it is to
be observed that two things are promised to Abraham, the
one, that his seed should possess the land of Canaan, which
is intimated when it is said, "Go into a land that I will show
thee, and I will make of thee a great nation"; but the other

far more excellent, not about the carnal but about that spiritual seed through which Abraham is the father, not of the one Israelite nation, but of all nations who follow the footprints of his faith, which was first promised in the words, "And in thee shall all tribes of the earth be blessed." (16)

"When Abram was ninety years old and nine, God appeared to him, and said unto him, 'I am the Almighty God; walk before me and be thou perfect. And I will make my covenant between me and thee, and will multiply thee exceedingly.'" (Gen. 17, 1–2) (26)

After these things a son was born to Abraham, according to God's promise, of Sarah, and he was called Isaac. (31)

Isaac married Rebecca when he was forty years old, that is, in the 140th year of his father's life, three years after his mother's death. (33)

The continuation of the heavenly city in Abraham's descendants.

Let us now see how the times of the city of God run on from this point among Abraham's descendants. In the time from the first year of Isaac's life to the seventieth, when his sons were born, the only memorable thing is that when he prayed to God that his wife, who was barren, might bear, and the Lord granted what he sought, and she conceived, the twins leapt while still enclosed in her womb. And when she was troubled by this struggle and inquired of the Lord, she received this answer: "Two nations are in thy womb, and two manner of people shall be separated from thy bowels; and the one people shall be stronger than the other people, and the elder shall serve the younger." (Gen. 25, 23)

Isaac's two sons, Esau and Jacob, grew up together. The primacy of the elder was transferred to the younger by a bargain and agreement between them when the elder immoderately lusted after the lentils the younger had prepared for food, and for that price sold his birthright to him, confirming it with an oath.

Isaac grew old, and old age deprived him of his eyesight. He wished to bless the elder son, and instead of the elder, who was hairy, unwittingly blessed the younger, who put himself under his father's hands, having covered himself with kid-skins. But what is the blessing itself? "See," Isaac said, "the smell of my son is as the smell of a field which the Lord hath blessed: therefore God give thee of the dew of heaven, and of the fatness of the earth, and plenty of corn and wine: let nations serve thee, and princes adore thee: and be lord over thy brethren, and let thy father's sons adore thee: cursed be he that curseth thee, and blessed be he that blesseth thee." (Gen. 27, 27–29)

The blessing of Jacob is a proclamation of Christ to all nations. It is this which has come to pass and is now being fulfilled. Isaac's words are law and prophecy: even by the mouth of a Jew Christ is blessed by prophecy through one who knows not, because the prophecy itself is not understood. The world like a field is filled with the odor of Christ's name; His is the blessing of the dew of heaven, that is, of the showers of divine words; and of the fruitfulness of the earth, that is, of the gathering together of the peoples; His is the plenty of corn and wine, that is, the multitude that gathers bread and wine in the sacrament of His body and blood. Him the nations serve, Him princes adore. He is the Lord of His brethren, because His people rule over the Jews. Him His Father's sons adore, that is, the sons of Abraham according to faith; for He Himself is the son of Abraham according to the flesh. He is cursed that curses Him, and he that blesses Him is blessed. (37)

Jacob was sent by his parents to Mesopotamia that he might take a wife there. And the divine Scripture points out how, without unlawfully desiring any of them, he came to have four women, of whom he begat twelve sons [14] and one daughter. (38)

[14] The 12 sons of Jacob were named: Reuben, Simeon, Levi, Judah, Issachar, Zebulun, Joseph, Benjamin, Dan, Naphtali, Gad, and Asher. (Gen. 35, 23–26)

If, on account of the Christian people in whom the city of God sojourns on this earth, we look for the flesh of Christ in the seed of Abraham, we have Isaac; if in the seed of Isaac, we have Jacob, who also is Israel; if in the seed of Israel himself, we have Judah, because Christ sprang of the tribe of Judah. Let us hear, then, how Israel, when dying in Egypt, in blessing his sons, prophetically blessed Judah. He says "Judah is a lion's whelp. A prince shall not be lacking out of Judah, and a leader from his thighs, until the things come that are laid up for him; and He shall be the expectation of the nations." (Gen. 49, 9–10) (41)

During the remaining 144 years until they went out of the land of Egypt,[15] that nation increased to an incredible degree, even although wasted by so great persecutions that at one time the male children were murdered at their birth, because the wondering Egyptians were terrified at the too great increase of that people. Then Moses, being stealthily kept from the murderers of the infants, was brought to the royal house, God preparing to do great things by him, and was nursed and adopted by the daughter of Pharaoh (that was the name of all the kings of Egypt), and became so great a man that he—yea, rather God, who had promised this to Abraham, by him—drew that nation, so wonderfully multiplied, out of the yoke of hardest and most grievous servitude it had borne there.

Then for forty years the people of God went through the desert under the leadership of Moses. On the death of Moses, Joshua the son of Nun ruled the people and led them into the land of promise and divided it among them. By these two wonderful leaders wars were also carried on most prosperously and wonderfully, God calling to witness that they had got these victories not so much on account of the merit

[15] Jacob, during a period of famine, went with his family into Egypt, where Joseph, who had been sold into bondage by his brothers, had become Pharaoh's favorite adviser. Acquaintance with the story of Joseph and of the fate of the children of Israel in Egypt is taken for granted by Augustine and should be read: Gen. 37–50, and Ex. 1–14.

of the Hebrew people as on account of the sins of the nations they subdued. After these leaders there were judges, when the people were settled in the land of promise, so that, in the meantime, the first promise made to Abraham began to be fulfilled about the one nation, that is, the Hebrew, and about the land of Canaan; but not as yet the promise about all nations and the whole wide world, for that was to be fulfilled by the advent of Christ in the flesh.

We come next to the times of the kings. The first who reigned was Saul; and when he was rejected and laid low in battle, David succeeded to the kingdom, whose son Christ is chiefly called. (43)

BOOK XVII

The history of the heavenly city from David
to Christ

*David lived at the beginning of the prophetic age, and
many of his psalms clearly refer to Christ and His
Church.*

By the favor of God we have treated distinctly of His
promises made to Abraham, that both the nation of Israel
according to the flesh and all nations according to the faith
should be his seed; and the city of God, proceeding according to the order of time, has pointed out how they were fulfilled.

Having therefore in the previous book come down to the
reign of David, we shall now treat of what remains, so far as
may seem sufficient for the object of this work, beginning at
the same reign.

Now, from the time when holy Samuel [16] began to proph-
esy, and ever onward until the people of Israel was led captive into Babylonia, and until, on Israel's return thence after
seventy years, the house of God was built anew, this whole
period is *the prophetic age.*

If I wished to rehearse all that the prophets have predicted
concerning Christ while the city of God, with its members
dying and being born in constant succession, ran its course
through those times, this work would extend beyond all
bounds. Therefore I shall, if I can, so limit myself that, in
carrying through this work, I may, with God's help, neither
say what is superfluous nor omit what is necessary. (1)

In the progress of the city of God through the ages, David

[16] The prophet Samuel anointed Saul, the first king, and David, the
second king of the children of Israel.

first reigned in the earthly Jerusalem, a shadow of that Jerusalem which is to come. Now David was a man skilled in songs, who dearly loved musical harmony, not with a vulgar delight, but with a believing disposition, and by it served his God, who is the true God, by the symbolic representation of a great thing. For the rational and well-ordered concord of diverse sounds in harmonious variety suggests the compact unity of the well-ordered city. (14)

And now I see it may be expected of me that I shall open up in this part of this book what David may have prophesied in the Psalms concerning the Lord Jesus Christ or His Church. (15)

Some of them, indeed, on the very first blush, as soon as they are spoken, exhibit Christ and the Church:

"Thou art fairer than the children of men; grace is poured into thy lips: therefore God hath blessed thee for ever. Gird thy sword upon thy thigh, O most mighty . . . thy throne, O God, is for ever and ever." (Ps. 45, 2–6)

Who is there, no matter how slow, but must here recognize Christ whom we preach and in whom we believe, if he hears that He is God, whose throne is for ever and ever. Then let him look upon His Church, joined to her so great husband in spiritual marriage and divine love, of which it is said in the words which follow, "the queen stood upon Thy right hand in gold-embroidered vestments. Hearken, O daughter, and look, and incline thine ear; forget also thy people and thy father's house. Because the king has greatly desired thy beauty; for He is the Lord thy God." (Ps. 45, 9–11) I do not think anyone is so stupid as to believe that some poor woman is here praised and described, as the spouse, to wit, of Him to whom it is said, "Thy throne, O God, is for ever and ever . . . Thy God hath anointed Thee with the oil of gladness above Thy fellows" (Ps. 45, 9–17), which means that God has anointed Christ above the Christians. For they are His fellows, of whose concord and unity in all nations the queen—or as another psalm says, "The city of the great King"—is formed. (Ps. 48, 2) This queen is Jerusalem spiritually, of which we already have said many things. Her enemy is the city of the devil, Babylon. Yet out of this Babylon the queen is in all nations set free by regeneration, and passes from the worst to the best King, i.e., from the devil to Christ. Wherefore it is said to her, "Forget thy people and thy father's house." Of this impious city those are also a portion who are Israelites only in the flesh and not by faith, enemies also of this great King Himself and of His queen. (16)

Neither can it be denied that it is Christ speaking through David who utters through prophecy the humiliation of His passion, saying, "They pierced my hands and my feet; they counted all my bones. Yea, they looked and stared at me." (Ps. 22, 16–17) By which words he certainly meant His body stretched out on the cross, with the hands and feet pierced and perforated by the striking through of the nails, so that He had in that way made Himself a spectacle to those who looked and stared. And he adds, "They parted my garments among them, and over my vesture they cast lots." (Ps. 22, 18) How this prophecy has been fulfilled the Gospel history narrated. (17)

But the Jews do not expect that the Christ whom they expect will die; therefore they do hold not ours to be Him whom the law and the prophets announced, but some one, I know not whom, of their own, whom they imagine to be exempt from the suffering of death. But the 16th Psalm also cries to them, "My flesh also shall rest in hope; for Thou wilt not leave my soul in hell; neither wilt Thou suffer Thine Holy One to see corruption." (Ps. 16, 9) Who but He that rose again the third day could say His flesh had rested in this hope; that His soul, not being left in hell, but speedily returning to His body, should revive it so that it should not be corrupted as corpses are wont to be, which they can in no wise say of David the prophet and king? (18)

David was succeeded by Solomon. After Solomon, the kingdom declined until Christ found the Hebrews paying tribute to Rome.

David reigned in the earthly Jerusalem, a son of the heavenly Jerusalem, much praised by divine testimony; for even his faults are overcome by great piety through the most salutary humility of his repentance, so that he is altogether one of those to whom he himself says, "Blessed are they whose iniquities are forgiven, and whose sins are covered." (Ps. 32, 1)

After him Solomon his son reigned over the same whole people. This man, after good beginnings, made a bad end. For indeed "Prosperity, which wears out the minds of the wise," [17] hurt him more than that wisdom profited him which even yet is and shall hereafter be renowned, and was then praised far and wide. (20)

The other kings of the Hebrews after Solomon are scarcely found to have prophesied what may pertain to Christ and the Church, either in Judah or in Israel; for so were the parts of that kingdom called, when, from the time of Rehoboam, Solomon's son, who succeeded Solomon in the kingdom, this kingdom, on account of Solomon's offence, was divided by God as a punishment. The ten tribes which Jeroboam, the servant of Solomon received, being appointed the king in Samaria, were distinctively called Israel, although this had been the name of that whole people; but the two tribes Judah and Benjamin, which for David's sake—lest the kingdom should be wholly wrenched from his race—remained subject to the city of Jerusalem, were called Judah, because that was the tribe whence David sprang. On the division of the people, therefore, Rehoboam, son of Solomon, reigned in Jerusalem as the first king of Judah, and Jeroboam, servant of Solomon, in Samaria as king of Israel. (21)

Each part, as the divine providence either ordered or permitted, was both lifted up by prosperity and weighed down by adversity of various kinds; and it was afflicted not only by foreign but also by civil wars with each other in order that by certain existing causes the mercy or anger of God might be

[17] Quoted from Sallust, see Note (5).

manifested; until, by His growing indignation, that whole nation was by conquering Chaldeans not only overthrown in its abode, but also for the most part transported to the lands of the Assyrians—first, that part called Israel, but afterwards Judah also, when Jerusalem and that most noble temple was cast down—in which lands it rested seventy years in captivity. Being after that time sent forth thence, they rebuilt the overthrown temple. And although very many stayed in the lands of the strangers, yet the kingdom no longer had two separate parts with different kings over each, but in Jerusalem there was one prince over them; and at certain times, from every direction wherever they were, and from whatever place they could, they all came to the temple of God which was there. Yet not even then were they without foreign enemies and conquerors; yea, Christ found them tributaries of the Romans. (23)

BOOK XVIII

The parallel courses of the earthly and heavenly
cities from Abraham to the end of the world

Summary of the first seventeen books.

I promised to write of the rise, progress, and appointed
end of the two cities, one of which is God's, the other this
world's, in which, so far as mankind is concerned, the former
is now a stranger. But first of all I undertook, so far as His
grace should enable me, to refute the enemies of the city of
God, who prefer their gods to Christ, its founder, and fiercely
hate Christians with the most deadly malice. And this I have
done in the first ten books. Then, as regards my threefold
promise which I have just mentioned, I have treated distinctly, in the four books which follow the tenth, of the rise
of both cities. After that, I have proceeded from the first
man down to the flood in one book, which is the fifteenth of
this work; and from that again down to Abraham our work
has followed both cities in chronological order. From the
patriarch Abraham down to the time of the Israelite kings, at
which we close our sixteenth book, and thence down to the
advent of Christ Himself in the flesh, to which period the
seventeenth book reaches, the city of God appears from
my way of writing to have run its course alone; whereas it
did not run its course alone in this age, for both cities, in
their course amid mankind, certainly experienced chequered
times together just as from the beginning. But I did this in
order that, first of all, from the time when the promises of
God began to be more clear down to the virgin birth of Him
in whom those things promised from the first were to be fulfilled, the course of that city which is God's might be made

more distinctly apparent, without interpolation of foreign matter from the history of the other city, although down to the revelation of the new covenant it ran its course, not in light, but in shadow. Now, therefore, I think fit to do what I passed by, and show, so far as seems necessary, how that other city ran its course from the times of Abraham, so that attentive readers may compare the two. (1)

Assyria, Rome, and the Jewish prophets.

Among the very many kingdoms of the earth into which, by earthly interest or lust, that society is divided which we call by the general name of the city of this world, we see that two, settled and kept distant from each other both in time and place, have grown far more famous than the rest, first that of the Assyrians, then that of the Romans. First came the one, then the other. The former arose in the east, and, immediately on its close, the latter in the west. (2)

The city of Rome was founded like another Babylon, and as it were the daughter of the former Babylon, by which God was pleased to conquer the whole world and subdue it far and wide by bringing it into one fellowship of government and laws. But there were now already powerful and brave peoples and nations trained to arms, who did not easily yield, and whose subjection necessarily involved great danger and destruction as well as great and horrible labour. For when the Assyrian kingdom subdued almost all Asia, although this was done by fighting, yet the wars could not be very fierce or difficult, because the nations were as yet untrained to resist, and neither so many nor so great as afterward. But Rome did not with the same quickness and facility wholly subdue all those nations of the east and west which we see brought under the Roman empire, because, in its gradual increase, in whatever direction it was extended, it found them strong and warlike. (22)

When Zedekiah reigned over the Hebrews, and Tarquinius

Priscus [18] over the Romans, the Jewish people was led captive into Babylon.[19] (25)

Cyrus,[20] king of Persia, who also ruled the Chaldeans and Assyrians, having somewhat relaxed the captivity of the Jews, made fifty thousand of them return in order to rebuild the temple. They only began the first foundations and built the altar; but, owing to hostile invasions, they were unable to go on, and the work was put off to the time of Darius. Under Darius, king of Persia, the captivity of the Jews was brought to an end, and they were restored to liberty. Tarquin then reigned as the seventh king of the Romans. On his expulsion, they also began to be free from the rule of their kings. Down to this time the people of Israel had prophets; but although they were numerous, the canonical writings of only a few of them have been preserved among the Jews and among us. (26)

The Septuagint and Vulgate versions of the Scriptures.

One of the Ptolemies, kings of Egypt, desired to know and have these sacred books. For after Alexander of Macedon, who is also named the Great, had by his most wonderful, but by no means enduring power, subdued the whole of Asia, yea, almost the whole world, partly by force of arms, partly by terror, and, among other kingdoms of the East, had entered and obtained Judea also, his generals, on his death, did not peaceably divide that most ample kingdom among them for a possession, but rather dissipated it, wasting all things by wars. Then Egypt began to have the Ptolemies as her kings. The first of them, the son of Lagus, carried many captive out of Judea into Egypt. But another Ptolemy, called Philadelphus, who succeeded him,[21] permitted all whom he

[18] The fifth king.

[19] First conquest of Jerusalem took place in 597; it was destroyed in 587.

[20] In 539 B.C., Cyrus, the Persian, conquers Babylon and founds the great Persian Empire.

[21] In 285 B.C.

had brought under the yoke to return free; and, more than that, sent kingly gifts to the temple of God, and begged Eleazar, who was the high priest, to give him the Scriptures, which he had heard by report were truly divine, and therefore greatly desired to have in that most noble library he had made. When the high priest had sent them to him in Hebrew, he afterwards demanded interpreters of him, and there were given him seventy-two, out of each of the twelve tribes six men most learned in both languages, to wit, the Hebrew and Greek; and their translation is now by custom called the Septuagint. It is reported, indeed, that there was an agreement in their words so wonderful, stupendous, and plainly divine, that when they had sat at this work, each one apart —for so it pleased Ptolemy to test their fidelity—they differed from each other in no word which had the same meaning and force, or in the order of the words; but, as if the translators had been one, so what all had translated was one, because in very deed the one Spirit had been in them all. And they received so wonderful a gift of God in order that the authority of these Scriptures might be commended not as human but divine, as indeed it was, for the benefit of the nations who should at some time believe, as we now see them doing. (42)

For while there were other interpreters who translated these sacred oracles out of the Hebrew tongue into Greek, yet the Church has received this Septuagint translation just as if it were the only one; and it has been used by the Greek Christian people, most of whom are not aware that there is any other. From this translation there has also been made a translation in the Latin tongue, which the Latin churches use. Our times, however, have enjoyed the advantage of the presbyter Jerome, a man most learned, and skilled in all three languages, who translated these same Scriptures into the Latin speech, not from the Greek, but from the Hebrew. (43)

The birth, death, and resurrection of Christ.

While Herod reigned in Judea, and Caesar Augustus was emperor at Rome, the state of the republic being already changed, and the world being set at peace by him, Christ was born in Bethlehem of Judah, man manifest out of a human virgin, God hidden out of God the Father. For so had the prophet foretold: "Behold, a virgin shall conceive in the womb, and bring forth a Son, and they shall call His name Immanuel, which, being interpreted, is, God with us." (Gen. 49, 10) He did many miracles that He might commend God in Himself, some of which, even as many as seemed sufficient to proclaim Him, are contained in the evangelic Scripture. The first of these is that He was so wonderfully born, and the last that, with His body raised up again from the dead, He ascended into heaven. But the Jews who slew Him and would not believe in Him, because it behooved Him to die and rise again, were yet more miserably wasted by the Romans and utterly rooted out from their kingdom, where aliens had already ruled over them, and were dispersed through the lands. (46)

The spread of Christianity.

In this wicked world, in these evil days, when the Church measures her future loftiness by her present humility and is exercised by goading fears, tormenting sorrows, disquieting labors, and dangerous temptations, when she soberly rejoices, rejoicing only in hope, there are many reprobate mingled with the good, and both are gathered together by the gospel as in a dragnet; and in this world, as in a sea, both swim enclosed without distinction in the net, until it is brought ashore, when the wicked must be separated from the good, that in the good, as in His temple, God may be all in all.

We acknowledge, indeed, that His word is now fulfilled who spake in the psalm, and said, "I have announced and spoken; they are multiplied above number." (Ps. 40, 5) This takes place now, since He has spoken, first by the mouth of his forerunner John, and afterward by His own mouth, saying, "Repent: for the kingdom of heaven is at hand." (Matt. 3, 2) He chose disciples, whom He also called apostles, of lowly birth, unhonored, and illiterate, so that whatever great thing they might do, He might be and do it in them. He had one among them whose wickedness He could use well in order to accomplish His appointed passion and furnish His Church an example of bearing with the wicked. Having sown the holy gospel as much as that behoved to be done by His bodily presence, He suffered, died, and rose again, showing by His passion what we ought to suffer for the truth, and by His resurrection what we ought to hope for in adversity; saving always the mystery of the sacrament, by which His blood was shed for the remission of sins. He held converse on the earth forty days with His disciples, and in their sight ascended into heaven, and after ten days sent the promised Holy Spirit. It was given as the chief and most necessary sign of His coming on those who had believed, that every one of them spoke in the tongues of all nations; thus signifying that the unity of the catholic Church would embrace all nations, and would in like manner speak in all tongues. (49)

Then was fulfilled that prophecy, "Out of Sion shall go forth the law, and the word of the Lord out of Jerusalem"; (Isa. 2, 3) and the prediction of the Lord Christ Himself, when, after the resurrection, "He opened the understanding" of His amazed disciples "that they might understand the Scriptures, and said unto them that thus it is written, and thus it behoved Christ to suffer, and to rise from the dead the third day, and that repentance and remission of sins should be preached in His name among all nations beginning at Jerusalem." (Luke 24, 45–47) And again, when, in reply to their questioning about the day of His last coming, He said, "It is not for you to know the times or the seasons which the Father hath put in His own power; but ye shall receive the power of the Holy Ghost coming upon you, and ye shall be witnesses unto me both in Jerusalem, and in all Judea, and

Samaria, and even unto the ends of the earth." (Acts 1, 7–8)

First of all, the Church spread herself abroad from Jerusalem; and when very many in Judea and Samaria had believed, she also went into other nations by those who announced the gospel, whom, as lights, He Himself had both prepared by His word and kindled by His Holy Spirit. For He had said to them, "Fear ye not them which kill the body, but are not able to kill the soul." (Matt. 10, 28) And that they might not be frozen with fear, they burned with the fire of charity. Finally, the gospel of Christ was preached in the whole world, not only by those who had seen and heard Him both before His passion and after His resurrection, but also after their death by their successors, amid horrible persecutions, diverse torments and deaths of the martyrs, God also bearing them witness, both with signs and wonders and divers miracles and gifts of the Holy Ghost, that the people of the nations, believing in Him who was crucified for their redemption, might venerate with Christian love the blood of the martyrs which they had poured forth with devilish fury. (50)

Thus in this world, in these evil days, not only from the time of the bodily presence of Christ and His apostles, but even from that of Abel, whom first his wicked brother slew because he was righteous, and thenceforth even to the end of this world, the Church has gone forward on pilgrimage amid the persecutions of the world and the consolations of God. (51)

The coming persecution of the Church during the reign of Antichrist, which will precede the end of this world.

I do not think that until the time of Antichrist the Church of Christ is not to suffer any persecutions besides those she has already suffered—that is, ten—and that the eleventh and last shall be inflicted by Antichrist. It does not seem to me that the number of persecutions with which the Church is to be tried can be definitely stated. (52)

Truly Jesus Himself shall extinguish by His presence that last persecution which is to be made by Antichrist. For so it is written, that "He shall slay him with the breath of His mouth, and empty him with the brightness of His presence." (Isa. 11, 4; II Thess. 1, 9) It is customary to ask, When shall that be? But this is quite unreasonable. For had it been profitable for us to know this, by whom could it better have been told than by God Himself, the Master, when the disciples questioned Him? For they were not silent when with Him, but inquired of Him, saying, "Lord, wilt Thou at this time present the kingdom to Israel, or when?" (Acts 1, 6–7) But He said, "It is not for you to know the times, which the Father hath put in His own power."

In vain, then, do we attempt to compute definitely the years that may remain to this world, when we may hear from the mouth of the Truth that it is not for us to know this. Yet some have said that four hundred, some five hundred, others a thousand years, may be completed from the ascension of the Lord up to His final coming. But on this subject He puts aside the figures of the calculators and orders silence who says, "It is not for you to know the times, which the Father hath put in His own power." (53)

But let us now at last finish this book, after thus far treating of, and showing as far as seemed sufficient, what is the mortal course of the two cities, the heavenly and the earthly, which are mingled together from the beginning down to the end. Of these, the earthly one has made to herself false gods whom she might serve by sacrifice; but she which is heavenly, and is a pilgrim on the earth, does not make false gods, but is herself made by the true God, of whom she herself must be the true sacrifice. Yet both alike either enjoy temporal good things or are afflicted with temporal evils, but with diverse faith, diverse hope, and diverse love, until they must be separated by the last judgment, and each must receive her own end, of which there is no end. About these ends of both we must next treat. (54)

BOOK XIX

The end of the two cities and the value of civic
peace for both cities

*The supreme good, the only justification of philos-
ophy, cannot be attained in this life.*

As I see that I have still to discuss the fit destinies of the
two cities, the earthly and the heavenly, I must first explain,
so far as the limits of this work allow me, the reasonings by
which men have attempted to make for themselves a happiness in this unhappy life, in order that it may be evident, not
only from divine authority, but also from such reasons as can
be adduced to unbelievers, how the empty dreams of philosophers differ from the hope which God gives to us, and
from the substantial fulfilment of it which He will give us as
our blessedness.

Philosophers have expressed a great variety of diverse
opinions regarding the ends of goods and of evils, and this
question they have eagerly canvassed, that they might, if possible, discover what makes a man happy. For the end of our
good is that for the sake of which other things are to be desired, while it itself is to be desired for its own sake; and the
end of evil is that on account of which other things are to be
shunned, while it itself is avoided on its own account. Thus,
by the end of good, we at present mean not that by which
good is destroyed, so that it no longer exists, but that by
which it is finished, so that it becomes complete; and by the
end of evil we mean not that which abolishes it, but that
which completes its development. These two ends, therefore,
are the supreme good and the supreme evil; and, as I have
said, those who have in this vain life professed the study of
wisdom have been at great pains to discover these ends, and

to obtain the supreme good and avoid the supreme evil in this life.

For man has no other reason for philosophizing than that he may be happy; but that which makes him happy is itself the supreme good. In other words, the supreme good is the reason of philosophizing. (1) If, then, we be asked what the city of God has to say upon these points, and, in the first place, what its opinion regarding the supreme good and evil is, it will reply that life eternal is the supreme good, that death eternal is the supreme evil, and that to obtain the one and escape the other we must live rightly. And thus it is written, "The just lives by faith," (Hab. 2, 4) for we do not as yet see our good, and must therefore live by faith; neither have we in ourselves power to live rightly, but can do so only if He who has given us faith to believe in His help does help us when we believe and pray. As for those who have supposed that the sovereign good and evil are to be found in this life, and have placed it either in the soul, or in the body, or in both, or, to speak more explicitly, either in pleasure, or in virtue, or in both—all these have, with a marvellous shallowness, sought to find their blessedness in this life and in themselves. (4)

The supreme good can be defined as "eternal life in peace" or as "peace in eternal life."

Here, indeed, we are said to be blessed when we have such peace as can be enjoyed in a good life; but such blessedness is mere misery compared to that final felicity. When we mortals possess such peace as this mortal life can afford, then virtue, if we are living rightly, makes a right use of the advantages of this peaceful condition; and when we have it not, virtue makes a good use even of the evils a man suffers. But this is a true virtue, when it refers all the advantages it makes a good use of, and all that it does in making good use of good and evil things, and itself also, to that end in which we shall enjoy the best and greatest peace possible. (10)

We may say of peace, as we have said of eternal life, that it is the end of our good. But as the word "peace" is employed in connection with things in this world in which certainly life eternal has no place, we have preferred to call the end or supreme good of this city "life eternal" rather than "peace." Of this end the apostle says, "But now, being freed from sin, and become servants to God, ye have your fruit unto holiness, and the end life eternal." (Rom. 6, 22) But, on the other hand, as those who are not familiar with Scripture may suppose that the life of the wicked is eternal life, either because of the immortality of the soul, which some of the philosophers even have recognized, or because of the endless punishment of the wicked, which forms a part of our faith and which seems impossible unless the wicked live for ever, it may therefore be advisable, in order that every one may readily understand what we mean, to say that the end or supreme good of this city is either "peace in eternal life," or "eternal life in peace." For peace is a good so great, that even in this earthly and mortal life there is no word we hear with such pleasure, nothing we desire with such zest, or find to be more thoroughly gratifying. (11)

The peace of the body consists in the duly proportioned arrangement of its parts. The peace of the irrational soul is the harmonious repose of the appetites, and the peace of the rational soul is the harmony of knowledge and action. The peace of body and soul is the well-ordered and harmonious life and health of the living creature. Peace between man and God is the well-ordered obedience of faith to eternal law. Peace between man and man is well-ordered concord. Domestic peace is the well-ordered concord between those of the family who rule and those who obey. Civil peace is a similar concord among the citizens. The peace of the celestial city is the perfectly ordered and harmonious enjoyment of God, and of one another in God. The peace of all things is the tranquillity of order. Order is the distribution which allots things equal and unequal, each to its own place. And hence, though the miserable, in so far as they are such, do certainly not enjoy peace, but are severed from that tranquillity of order in which there is no disturbance, nevertheless, inasmuch as they are deservedly and justly miserable, they are by their very misery connected with order. They are not, indeed, conjoined with the blessed, but they are disjoined from them by the law of order. And though they are disquieted, their circumstances are not withstanding adjusted to them, and consequently they have some tranquillity or order, and therefore some peace. (13)

The peace of the earthly city, in itself a legitimate good, must be supported by the city of God.

The families which do not live by faith seek their peace in the earthly advantages of this life; while the families which live by faith look for those eternal blessings which are promised, and use as pilgrims such advantages of time and of earth as do not fascinate and divert them from God but rather aid them to endure with greater ease, and to keep down the number of, those burdens of the corruptible body which weigh upon the soul. Thus the things necessary for this mortal life are used by both kinds of men and families alike, but each has its own peculiar and widely different aim in using them. The earthly city, which does not live by faith, seeks an earthly peace; and the end it proposes in the well ordered concord of civic obedience and rule is the combination of men's wills to attain the things which are helpful to this life. The heavenly city, or rather that part of it which sojourns on earth and lives by faith, makes use of this peace only because it must, until this mortal condition which necessitates it shall pass away. Consequently, as long as it lives like a captive and a stranger in the earthly city, though it has already received the promise of redemption and the gift of the Spirit as a seal of this promise, this city makes no scruple to obey the laws of the earthly city whereby the things necessary for the maintenance of this mortal life are administered;

and thus, as this life is common to both cities, there is harmony between them in regard to what belongs to it.

But, as the earthly city has had some philosophers who supposed that many gods must be invited to take an interest in human affairs, it has come to pass that the two cities could not have common laws of religion, and that the heavenly city has been compelled in this matter to dissent, to become obnoxious to those who think differently, and to stand the brunt of their anger and hatred and persecutions, except in so far as the minds of their enemies have been alarmed by the multitude of the Christians and quelled by the manifest protection of God accorded to them.

This heavenly city, then, while it sojourns on earth, calls citizens out of all nations, and gathers together a society of pilgrims of all languages, not scrupling about diversities in the manners, laws, and institutions whereby earthly peace is secured and maintained, but recognizing that, however various these are, they all tend to one and the same end of earthly peace. It therefore is so far from rescinding and abolishing these diversities that it even preserves and adopts them, so long only as no hindrance to the worship of the one supreme and true God is thus introduced. Even the heavenly city, therefore, while in its state of pilgrimage, avails itself of the peace of earth, and, so far as it can without injuring faith and godliness, desires and maintains a common agreement among men regarding the acquisition of the necessaries of life. (17)

Since, then, the supreme good of the city of God is perfect and eternal peace, not such as mortals pass into and out of by birth and death, but the peace of freedom from all evil, in which the immortals ever abide, who can deny that that future life is most blessed, or that, in comparison with it, this life which now we live is most wretched, be it filled with all blessings of body and soul and external things? And yet, if any man uses this life with a reference to that other which he ardently loves and confidently hopes for, he may well be called even now blessed, though not in reality so much as in hope. But the actual possession of the happiness of this life, without the hope of what is beyond, is but a false happiness and profound misery. (20)

Miserable, therefore, is the people which is alienated from God. Yet even this people has a peace of its own which is not to be lightly esteemed, though, indeed, it shall not in the end enjoy it, because it makes no good use of it before the end. But it is our interest that it enjoy this peace meanwhile in this life; for as long as the two cities are commingled, we also enjoy the peace of Babylon. And therefore the apostle also admonished the Church to pray for kings and those in authority, assigning as the reason, "that we may live a quiet and tranquil life in all godliness and love." (I Tim. 2, 2) And the prophet Jeremiah, when predicting the captivity that was to befall the ancient people of God, and giving them the divine command to go obediently to Babylonia and thus serve their God, counselled them also to pray for Babylonia, saying, "In the peace thereof shall ye have peace." (Jer. 29, 7)—the temporal peace which the good and the wicked together enjoy. (26)

But in that final peace to which all our righteousness has reference and for the sake of which it is maintained, as our nature shall enjoy a sound immortality and incorruption and shall have no more vices, and as we shall experience no resistance either from ourselves or from others, it will not be necessary that reason should rule vices which no longer exist, but God shall rule the man, and the soul shall rule the body, and obedience shall there be as pleasant and easy as the living and reigning with Christ will be blessed. And this condition shall there be eternal, and we shall be assured of its eternity; and thus the peace of this blessedness and the blessedness of this peace shall be the supreme good. (27)

But, on the other hand, they who do not belong to this city of God shall inherit eternal misery, which is also called the second death, because the soul shall then be separated from God its life, and therefore cannot be said to live, and the body shall be subjected to eternal pains. And consequently this second death shall be the more severe, because no death shall terminate it.

Now, as it is through the last judgment that men pass to these ends, the good to the supreme good, the evil to the supreme evil, I will treat of this judgment in the following book. (28)

BOOK XX

The last judgment and the final separation of
the two cities

On the day of the last judgment, the justice of God,
now often concealed, will be apparent to all.

In this book I shall speak, as God permits, of the last judgment, when Christ is to come from heaven to judge the quick
and the dead. For that day is properly called the day of
judgment, because in it there shall be no room left for the
ignorant questioning why this wicked person is happy and
that righteous man unhappy. In that day true and full happiness shall be the lot of none but the good, while deserved
and supreme misery shall be the portion of the wicked, and
of them only. (1)

In this present time we learn to bear with equanimity the
ills to which even good men are subject, and to hold cheap
the blessings which even the wicked enjoy. And consequently, even in those conditions of life in which the justice
of God is not apparent, His teaching is salutary. For we do
not know by what judgment of God this good man is poor
and that bad man rich; why he who, in our opinion, ought to
suffer acutely for his abandoned life enjoys himself, while
sorrow pursues him whose praiseworthy life leads us to suppose he should be happy.

But when we shall have come to that judgment the date
of which is called specifically "the day of judgment" and
sometimes "the day of the Lord," we shall then recognize the
justice of all God's judgments. And in that day we shall also
recognize with what justice so many, or almost all, the just
judgments of God in the present life defy the scrutiny of

human sense or insight, though in this matter it is not concealed from pious minds that what is concealed is just. (2)

The Scriptures prove that there will be a last judgment
on the day of the resurrection of the dead.

The proofs of this last judgment of God which I propose to adduce shall be drawn first from the New Testament, and then from the Old. For although the Old Testament is prior in point of time, the New has the precedence in intrinsic value; for the Old acts the part of herald to the New. (4)

The Saviour Himself, while reproving the cities in which He had done great works but which had not believed, and while setting them in unfavorable comparison with foreign cities, says, "Verily, I say unto you: 'It shall be more tolerable for the land of Sodom in the day of judgment than for thee.'" (Matt. 11, 24) Here He most plainly predicts that a day of judgment is to come. And in another place He says, "The men of Nineveh shall rise in judgment with this generation, and shall condemn it: because they repented at the preaching of Jonas; and, behold, a greater than Jonas is here. The queen of the south shall rise up in the judgment with this generation, and shall condemn it: for she came from the uttermost parts of the earth to hear the words of Solomon; and behold, a greater than Solomon is here." (Matt. 12, 41–42) Two things we learn from this passage: that a judgment is to take place, and that it is to take place at the resurrection of the dead. For when He spoke of the Ninevites and the queen of the south, He certainly spoke of dead persons, and yet He said that they should rise up in the day of judgment.

Moreover, the evangelist John most distinctly states that Christ had predicted that the judgment should be at the resurrection of the dead. For after saying, "The Father judgeth no man, but hath committed all judgment unto the Son; that all men should honor the Son, even as they honor the Father: he that honoreth not the Son, honoreth not the Father which hath sent Him," Christ immediately adds, "Verily, verily, I say unto you, He that heareth my word and believeth on Him that sent me, hath everlasting life, and shall not come into judgment; but is passed from death to life." (John 5, 22–24) How, then, shall they be separated from the wicked by judgment and be set at His right hand, unless "judgment" is in this passage used for "condemnation"? For into judgment, in this sense, they shall not come who hear His word and believe on Him that sent Him. (5)

The regeneration of sinners may be called the "first resurrection," while the term "second resurrection" should be used for the resurrection of the body on the day of the last judgment.

After that He adds the words, "Verily, verily, I say unto you, The hour is coming and now is, when the dead shall hear the voice of the Son of God; and they that hear shall live." (John 5, 25) As yet He does not speak of the second resurrection, that is, the resurrection of the body, which shall be in the end, but of the first, which is *now*. It is for the sake of making this distinction that He says, "The hour is coming, and now is." Now this resurrection regards not the body, but the soul. For souls, too, have a death of their own in wickedness and sins whereby they are the dead of whom the same lips say, "Suffer the dead to bury their dead," (Matt. 8, 22) —that is, let those who are dead in soul bury them that are dead in body. It is of these dead, then, the dead in ungodliness and wickedness, that He says, "The hour is coming, and now is, when the dead shall hear the voice of the Son of God; and they that hear shall live." "They that hear," that is, they who obey, believe, and persevere to the end. Here no difference is made between the good and the bad for it is good for all men to hear His voice and live by passing to the life of godliness from the death of ungodliness. Of this death the Apostle Paul says, "Therefore all are dead, and He died for all, that they which live should not henceforth live unto themselves, but unto Him which died for them and rose again." (2. Cor. 5, 14–15) Thus all, without one exception, were dead in sins, whether original or voluntary sins, sins of ignorance, or sins committed against knowledge; and for all the dead there died the one only person who lived, that is, who had no sin whatever, in order that they who live by the remission of their sins should live, not to themselves, but to Him who died for all, for our sins, and rose again for our justification, that we, believing in Him, may be able to attain to the first resurrection which now is. For in this first resurrection none have a part save those who shall be eternally blessed; but in the second, as we shall learn, have a part both the blessed and the wretched. The one is a resurrection of mercy, the other of judgment.

So there are two resurrections—the one the first and spiritual resurrection, which has place in this life and preserves us from coming into the second death; the other the second, which does not occur now, but in the end of the world, and which is of the body, not of the soul, and which by the last judgment shall dismiss some into the second death, others into that life which has no death. (6)

St. John is often misunderstood: there will be no "second coming" of Christ for the establishment of the millennium and then a "third coming" on judgment day, but only a second coming on the day of the last judgment. The millennium is now.

The evangelist John has spoken of these two resurrections in the book which is called the Apocalypse, but in such a way that some Christians do not understand the first of the two and so construe the passage into ridiculous fancies. For the Apostle John says in the foresaid book, "And I saw an angel come down from heaven, having the key of the bottomless pit and a great chain in his hand. And he laid hold on the dragon, that old serpent, which is the Devil and Satan, and bound him a thousand years. And cast him into the bottomless pit, and shut him up, and set a seal upon him, that he should deceive the nations no more, till the thousand years should be fulfilled: and after that he must be loosed a little season.

And I saw thrones, and they sat upon them, and judgment was given unto them: and I saw the souls of them that were beheaded for the witness of Jesus, and for the word of God, and which had not worshipped the beast, neither his image, neither had received his mark upon their foreheads, or in their hands; and they lived and reigned with Christ a thousand years.

But the rest of the dead lived not again until the thousand years were finished. This is the first resurrection. Blessed and holy is he that hath part in the first resurrection: on such the second death hath no power, but they shall be priests of God and of Christ, and shall reign with Him a thousand years." (Rev. 20, 1–6)

By the bottomless pit is meant the countless multitude of the wicked whose hearts are unfathomably deep in malignity against the Church of God; not that the devil was not there before, but he is said to be cast in thither, because, when prevented from harming believers, he takes more complete possession of the ungodly. For that man is more abundantly possessed by the devil who is not only alienated from God, but also gratuitously hates those who serve God. "And shut him up, and set a seal upon him, that he should deceive the nations no more till the thousand years should be fulfilled." "Shut him up"—i.e., prohibited him from going out, from doing what was forbidden. And the addition of "set a seal upon him" seems to me to mean that it was designed to keep it a secret who belonged to the devil's party and who did not. For in this world this is a secret, for we cannot tell whether even the man who seems to stand shall fall, or whether he who seems to lie shall rise again. But by the chain and prison-house of this interdict the devil is prohibited and restrained from seducing those nations which belong to Christ, but which he formerly seduced or held in subjection. For before the foundation of the world God chose to rescue these from

the power of darkness, and to translate them into the kingdom of the Son of His Love. For what Christian is not aware
that he seduces nations even now, and draws them with
himself to eternal punishment, but not those predestined to
eternal life? And let no one be dismayed by the circum-
stance that the devil often seduces even those who have been
regenerated in Christ, and begun to walk in God's way. For
"the Lord knoweth them that are His," (II Tim. 2, 19) and
of these the devil seduces none to eternal damnation. (7)

But while the devil is bound, the saints reign with Christ
during the same thousand years, i.e., between His first and
second coming. For, leaving out of account that kingdom
concerning which He shall say in the end, "Come, ye blessed
of my Father, take possession of the kingdom prepared for
you," (Matt. 25, 34) the Church could not now be called
His kingdom or the kingdom of heaven unless His saints were
even now reigning with Him.

From the Church "reapers" shall gather out the tares
which He suffered to grow with the wheat till the harvest, as
He explains in the words, "The harvest is the end of the
world; and the reapers are the angels. As therefore the tares
are gathered together and burned with fire, so shall it be in
the end of the world. The Son of man shall send His angels,
and they shall gather out of His kingdom all things that
offend." (Matt. 13, 39–41) Can He mean out of that eternal
kingdom in which are no offenses? Then it must be out of
His present kingdom, the Church, that they are gathered. So
He says, "He that breaketh one of the least of these commandments, and teacheth men so, shall be called least in the
kingdom of heaven: but he that doeth and teacheth thus shall
be called great in the kingdom of heaven." (Matt. 5, 19) He
speaks of both as being in the kingdom of heaven, both the
man who does not perform the commandments which He
teaches—for "to break" means not to keep, not to perform
—and the man who does and teaches as He did; but the one
He calls least, the other great.

We must understand in one sense the kingdom of heaven

in which exist together both he who breaks what he teaches and he who does it, the one being least, the other great, and in another sense the kingdom of heaven into which only he who does what he teaches shall enter. Consequently, where both classes exist, it is the Church as it now is, but where only the one shall exist, it is the Church as it is destined to be when no wicked person shall be in her. Therefore the Church even now is the kingdom of Christ and the kingdom of heaven. Accordingly, even now His saints reign with Him, though otherwise than as they shall reign hereafter.

It is then of this kingdom militant, in which conflict with the enemy is still maintained until we come to that most peaceful kingdom in which we shall reign without an enemy, and it is of this first resurrection in the present life, that the Apocalypse speaks in the words just quoted. For now is the hour when the dead shall hear the voice of the Son of God, and they that hear shall live; and the rest of them shall not live. Whosoever has not lived until the thousand years be finished, i.e., during this whole time in which the first resurrection is going on—whosoever has not heard the voice of the Son of God, and passed from death to life—that man shall certainly in the second resurrection, the resurrection of the flesh, pass with his flesh into the second death. For he goes on to say, "This is the first resurrection. Blessed and holy is he that hath part in the first resurrection," or who experiences it. Now he experiences it who not only revives from the death of sin, but continues in this renewed life. "In these the second death hath no power." Therefore it has power in the rest; for in this whole intervening time called a thousand years, however lustily this rest lived in the body, they were not quickened to life out of that death in which their wickedness held them, so that by this revived life they should become partakers of the first resurrection, and so the second death should have no power over them. (9)

The last persecution of the city of God during the reign of Antichrist.

"And when the thousand years are finished, Satan shall be loosed from his prison, and shall go out to seduce the nations which are in the four corners of the earth, Gog and Magog, and shall draw them to battle, whose number is as the sand of the sea." (Rev. 20, 7–8) This, then, is his purpose in seducing them, to draw them to this battle. For even before this he was wont to use as many and various seductions as he could continue. And the words "he shall go out" mean, he shall burst forth from lurking hatred into open persecution. For this persecution, occurring while the final judgment is imminent, shall be the last which shall be endured by the holy Church throughout the world, the whole city of Christ being assailed by the whole city of the devil, as each exists on earth. Gog and Magog are the nations in which we found that the devil was shut up as in an abyss, and the devil himself coming out from them and going forth from concealed to open hatred. The words, "And they went up on the breadth of the earth, and encompassed the camp of the saints and the beloved city," (Rev. 20, 9) do not mean that they have come, or shall come, to one place, as if the camp of the saints and the beloved city should be in some one place; for this camp is nothing else than the Church of Christ extending over the whole world. And consequently wherever the Church shall be—and it shall be in all nations, as is signified by "the breadth of the earth"—there also shall be the camp of the saints and the beloved city, and there it shall be encompassed by the savage persecution of all its enemies; for they too shall exist along with it in all nations. (11)

This last persecution by Antichrist shall last for three years and six months, as is affirmed both in the book of Revelation and by Daniel the prophet. Though this time is brief, yet not without reason is it questioned whether it is comprehended in the thousand years in which the devil is bound and the saints reign with Christ, or whether this little season should be added over and above to these years.

But who can dare to say that His members shall not reign

with Him at that very juncture when they shall most of all, and with the greatest fortitude, cleave to Him, and when the glory of resistance and the crown of martyrdom shall be more conspicuous in proportion to the hotness of the battle? Therefore during these three years and a half the souls of those who were slain for His testimony, both those which formerly passed from the body and those which shall pass in that last persecution, shall reign with Him till the mortal world come to an end, and pass into that kingdom in which there shall be no death. And thus the reign of the saints with Christ shall last longer than the bonds and imprisonment of the devil, because they shall reign with their King the Son of God for these three years and a half during which the devil is no longer bound.

After this mention of the closing persecution, St. John summarily indicates all that the devil, and the city of which he is the prince, shall suffer in the last judgment. For he says, "And the devil who seduced them is cast into the lake of fire and brimstone." (Rev. 20, 10)

After this he gives a brief narrative of the last judgment itself, which shall take place at the second or bodily resurrection of the dead, as it had been revealed to him: "I saw a throne great and white, and One sitting on it from whose face the heaven and the earth fled away, and their place was not found." (Rev. 20, 11) He does not say, "I saw a throne great and white, and One sitting on it, and from His face the heaven and the earth fled away," for it had not happened then, i.e., before the living and the dead were judged; but he says that he saw Him sitting on the throne from whose face heaven and earth fled away, but afterwards. For when the judgment is finished, this heaven and earth shall cease to be, and there will be a new heaven and a new earth.

"And I saw the dead, great and small: and the books were opened; . . . and they were judged every man according to their works." (Rev. 20, 12–13) (14)

The new heaven, the new earth, and the new Jerusalem.

As soon as those who are not written in the book of life have been judged and cast into eternal fire—the nature of which fire, or its position in the world or universe, I suppose is known to no man, unless perhaps the divine Spirit reveal it to someone—then shall the figure of this world pass away in a conflagration of universal fire, as once before the world was flooded with a deluge of universal water. And by this universal conflagration the qualities of the corruptible elements which suited our corruptible bodies shall utterly perish, and our substance shall receive such qualities as shall, by a wonderful transmutation, harmonize with our immortal bodies, so that, as the world itself is renewed to some better thing, it is fitly accommodated to men, themselves renewed in their flesh to some better thing. (16)

"And I saw," St. John says, "a great city, new Jerusalem, coming down from God out of heaven, prepared as a bride adorned for her husband. And I heard a great voice from the throne, saying, Behold, the tabernacle of God is with men, and He will dwell with them, and they shall be His people, and God Himself shall be with them. And God shall wipe away all tears from their eyes; and there shall be no more death, neither sorrow, nor crying, but neither shall there be any more pain: because the former things have passed away. And He that sat upon the throne said, Behold, I make all things new." (Rev. 21, 2–5) (17)

Someone will perhaps put the question, If after judgment is pronounced the world itself is to burn, where shall the saints be during the conflagration and before it is replaced by a new heaven and a new earth, since somewhere they must be, because they have material bodies? We may reply that they shall be in the upper regions into which the flame of that conflagration shall not ascend, as neither did the water of the flood; for they shall have such bodies that they shall be wherever they wish. Moreover, when they have become immortal and incorruptible, they shall not greatly dread the blaze of that conflagration. (18)

The fate of those Christians who are still living
when Christ comes to judge the quick and the dead.

The apostle, in his first Epistle to the Thessalonians, says, "But I would not have you to be ignorant, brethren, concerning them which are asleep, that ye sorrow not, even as others which have no hope. For if we believe that Jesus died and rose again, even so them also which sleep in Jesus will God bring with him.

For this we say unto you by the word of the Lord, that we which are alive and remain unto the coming of the Lord shall not prevent them which are asleep. For the Lord Himself shall descend from heaven with a shout, with the voice of the archangel, and with the trump of God; and the dead in Christ shall rise first." (I. Thess. 4, 13–16) These words of the apostle most distinctly proclaim the future resurrection of the dead, when the Lord Christ shall come to judge the quick and the dead.

But it is commonly asked whether those whom our Lord shall find alive upon earth, personated in this passage by the apostle and those who were alive with him, shall never die at all, or shall pass with incomprehensible swiftness through death to immortality in the very moment during which they shall be caught up along with those who rise again to meet the Lord in the air? For we cannot say that it is impossible that they should both die and revive again while they are carried aloft through the air. For the words, "And so shall we ever be with the Lord," are not to be understood as if he meant that we shall always remain in the air with the Lord; for He Himself shall not remain there, but shall only pass through it as He comes. For we shall go to meet Him as He comes, not where He remains; but "so shall we be with the Lord," that is, we shall be with Him possessed of immortal bodies wherever we shall be with Him. We seem compelled to take the words in this sense, and to suppose that those whom the Lord shall find alive upon earth shall in that brief space both suffer death and receive immortality. (20)

*The Jews will finally be converted and recognize Him
whom they have pierced.*

It is a familiar theme in the conversation and heart of the
faithful, that in the last days before the judgment the Jews
shall believe in the true Christ, that is, our Christ, by means
of this great and admirable prophet Elias who shall expound
the law to them. For not without reason do we hope that
before the coming of our Judge and Saviour, Elias shall
come, because we have good reason to believe that he is now
alive; for, as Scripture most distinctly informs us, (II Kings
2, 11), he was taken up from this life in a chariot of fire.
When, therefore, he is come, he shall give a spiritual ex-
planation of the law which the Jews at present understand
carnally. (29)

"And it shall come to pass in that day, that I will seek to
destroy all the nations that come against Jerusalem. And I
will pour upon the house of David, and upon the inhabitants
of Jerusalem, the spirit of grace and mercy; and they shall
look upon me because they have insulted me, and they shall
mourn for Him as for one very dear, and shall be in bitter-
ness as for an only-begotten." (Zech. 12, 9–10) To whom
but to God does it belong to destroy all the nations that are
hostile to the holy city Jerusalem; and yet Christ shows that
He is the God who does these so great and divine things,
when He goes on to say, "And they shall look upon me because they have insulted me, and they shall mourn for Him
as if for one very dear (or beloved), and shall be in bitter-
ness for Him as for an only-begotten." For in that day the
Jews—those of them, at least, who shall receive the spirit
of grace and mercy—when they see Him coming in His
majesty, shall repent of insulting Him in His passion: and
their parents themselves, who were the perpetrators of this
huge impiety, shall see Him when they rise; but this will be
only for their punishment, and not for their correction. It is
not of them we are to understand the words, "And I will
pour upon the house of David, and upon the inhabitants of

Jerusalem, the spirit of grace and mercy, and they shall look upon me because they have insulted me"; but we are to understand the words of their descendants, who shall at that time believe through Elias. Their grief shall arise not so much from guilt as from pious affection. Certainly the words which the Septuagint have translated, "They shall look upon me because they insulted me," stand in the Hebrew, "They shall look upon me whom they pierced." (30)

Summary

That the last judgment, then, shall be administered by Jesus Christ in the manner predicted in the sacred writings is denied or doubted by no one, unless by those who, through some incredible animosity or blindness, decline to believe these writings, though already their truth is demonstrated to all the world. And at or in connection with that judgment the following events shall come to pass, as we have learned: Elias shall come; the Jews shall believe; Antichrist shall persecute; Christ shall judge; the dead shall rise; the good and the wicked shall be separated; the world shall be burned and renewed. All these things, we believe, shall come to pass; but how, or in what order, human understanding cannot perfectly teach us, but only the experience of the events themselves. My opinion, however, is, that they will happen in the order in which I have related them.

Two books yet remain to be written by me, in order to complete, by God's help, what I promised. One of these will explain the punishment of the wicked, the other the happiness of the righteous.

BOOK XXI

Summary

The nature, the possibility, and the justice of eternal punishment

BOOK XXII

The nature of life eternal

The beauty of this present creation defies description, and it represents God's gift merely to those who have sinned.

This, the last book of the whole work, shall contain a discussion of the eternal blessedness of the city of God.

This blessedness is named eternal, not because it shall endure for many ages, though at last it shall come to an end, but because, according to the words of the gospel, "of His kingdom there shall be no end." (Luke 1, 33) Neither shall it enjoy the mere appearance of perpetuity which is maintained by the rise of fresh generations to occupy the place of those that have died out, as in an evergreen the same freshness seems to continue permanently, and the same appearance of dense foliage is preserved by the growth of fresh leaves in the room of those that have withered and fallen; but in that city all the citizens shall be immortal, men now for the first time enjoying what the holy angels have never lost. And this shall be accomplished by God, the most almighty Founder of the city.

For it is He who in the beginning created the world full of all visible and intelligible beings, among which He created nothing better than those spirits whom He endowed with intelligence and made capable of contemplating and enjoying Him.

It is He who gave to this intellectual nature free-will of such a kind, that if he wished to forsake God, i.e., his blessedness, misery should forthwith result. It is He who, when He foreknew that certain angels would in their pride desire to suffice for their own blessedness and would forsake their

121

great good, did not deprive them of this power, deeming it to be more befitting His power and goodness to bring good out of evil than to prevent the evil from coming into existence.

It is He who with very just punishment doomed the angels who voluntarily fell to everlasting misery, and rewarded those who continued in their attachment to the supreme good with the assurance of endless stability as the reward of their fidelity.

It is He who made also man himself upright, with the same freedom of will—an earthly animal, indeed, but fit for heaven if he remained faithful to his Creator, but destined to the misery appropriate to such a nature if he forsook Him.

It is He who, when He foreknew that man would in his turn sin by abandoning God and breaking His law, did not deprive him of the power of free will, because He at the same time foresaw what good He Himself would bring out of the evil and how from this mortal race, deservedly and justly condemned, He would by His grace collect, as now He does, a people so numerous that He thus fills up and repairs the blank made by the fallen angels, and that thus that beloved and heavenly city is not defrauded of the full number of its citizens, but perhaps may even rejoice in a still more over-flowing population. (1)

It is He, then, who has given to the human soul a mind in which reason and understanding lie, as it were, asleep during infancy as if they were not destined to be awakened and exercised as years increase so as to become capable of knowledge and of receiving instruction, fit to understand what is true and to love what is good. It is by this capacity that the soul drinks in wisdom and becomes endowed with those virtues by which, in prudence, fortitude, temperance, and righteousness, it makes war upon error and the other inborn vices, and conquers them by fixing its desires upon no other object than the supreme and unchangeable Good. And even though this be not uniformly the result, yet who can competently utter or even conceive the grandeur of this work of the Almighty and the unspeakable boon He has conferred upon our rational nature by giving us even the capacity of such attainment?

For over and above those arts which are called virtues, and which teach us how we may spend our life well and attain to endless happiness—arts which are given to the children of the kingdom by the sole grace of God which is in Christ —has not the genius of man invented and applied countless astonishing arts, partly the result of necessity, partly the result of exuberant invention, so that this vigor of mind, which is so active in the discovery not merely of superfluous but even of dangerous and destructive things, betokens an inexhaustible wealth in the nature which can invent, learn, or employ such arts? What wonderful—one might say stupefying—advances has human industry made in the arts of weaving and building, of agriculture and navigation! With what endless variety are designs in pottery, painting, and sculpture produced, and with what skill executed! What wonderful spectacles are exhibited in the theatres, which those who have not seen them cannot credit! How skillful the contrivances for catching, killing, or taming wild beasts! And for the injury of men, also, how many kinds of poisons, weapons, engines of destruction, have been invented, while for the preservation or restoration of health the appliances and remedies are infinite! To provoke appetite and please the palate, what a variety of seasonings have been concocted! To express and gain entrance for thoughts, what a multitude and variety of signs there are, among which speaking and writing hold the first place! what ornaments has eloquence at command to delight the mind! what wealth of song is there to captivate the ear! how many musical instruments and strains of harmony have been devised! What skill has been attained in measures and numbers! with what sagacity have the movements and connections of the stars been discovered!

Moreover, even in the body, though it dies like that of the beasts and is in many ways weaker than theirs, what goodness of God, what providence of the great Creator, is apparent! The organs of sense and the rest of the members, are not they so placed; the appearance, and form, and stature of the body as a whole, is it not so fashioned, as to indicate that it was made for the service of a reasonable soul? Man has not been created stooping towards the earth like the irrational animals; but his bodily form, erect and looking heavenwards, admonishes him to mind the things that are above. How can I tell of the rest of creation, with all its beauty and utility which the divine goodness has given to man to please his eye and serve his purposes, condemned though he is, and hurled into these labors and miseries? Shall I speak of the manifold and various loveliness of sky, and earth, and sea; of the plentiful supply and wonderful qualities of the light; of sun, moon, and stars; of the shade of trees; of the colors and perfume of flowers; of the multitude of birds, all differing in plumage and in song; of the variety of animals, of which the smallest in size are often the most wonderful —the works of ants and bees astonishing us more than the huge bodies of whales? Shall I speak of the sea, which itself is so grand a spectacle, when it arrays itself as it were in vestures of various colors, now running through every shade of green, and again becoming purple or blue? Is it not delightful to look at it in storm, and experience the soothing complacency which it inspires by suggesting that we ourselves are not tossed and shipwrecked?

Who can enumerate all the blessings we enjoy? If I were to attempt to detail and unfold only these few which I had indicated in the mass, such an enumeration would fill a volume. And all these are but the solace of the wretched and condemned, not the rewards of the blessed. What then shall these rewards be, if such be the blessings of a condemned state? What will He give to those whom He has predestined to life, who has given such things even to those whom He has predestined to death? In what condition shall the spirit of man be, when it has no longer any vice at all; when it neither yields to any, nor is in bondage to any, nor has to make war against any, but is perfected, and enjoys undisturbed peace with itself? Shall it not then know all things with certainty and without any labor or error, when unhindered and joyfully it drinks the wisdom of God at the fountain-head? (24)

What the blessed saints will experience when they see God as He is, is beyond our understanding.

And now let us consider how the saints shall be employed when they are clothed in immortal and spiritual bodies, and when the flesh shall live no longer in a fleshly but a spiritual fashion. And indeed, to tell the truth, I am at a loss to understand the nature of that employment or, shall I rather say, repose and ease, for it has never come within the range of my bodily senses. And if I should speak of my mind or understanding, what is our understanding in comparison to the excellence of this repose? For then shall be that "peace of God which," as the apostle says, "passeth all understanding." (Phil. 4, 7) Doubtless this passeth all understanding but His own. But we shall one day be made to participate, according to our slender capacity, in His peace. For we must remember how great a man he was who said, "Now we see through a glass, darkly; but then face to face." (I. Cor. 13, 12) Such also is now the vision of the holy angels. This vision is reserved as the reward of our faith; and of it the Apostle John also says, "When He shall appear, we shall be like Him, for we shall see Him as He is." (I John 3, 2) (29)

But who can conceive, not to say describe, what degrees of honor and glory shall be awarded to the various degrees of merit? Yet it cannot be doubted that there shall be degrees. And in that blessed city there shall be this great blessing that no inferior shall envy any superior, as now the archangels are not envied by the angels, because no one will wish to be what he has not received though bound in strictest concord with him who has received. And thus, along with his gift, greater or less, each shall receive this further gift of contentment to desire no more than he has.

Neither are we to suppose that because sin shall have no power to delight them, free will must be withdrawn. It will, on the contrary, be all the more truly free, because set free from delight in sinning to take unfailing delight in not sinning. For the first freedom of will, which man received when he was created upright, consisted in an ability not to sin, but also in an ability to sin; whereas this last freedom of will shall be superior, inasmuch as it shall not be able to sin. This, indeed, shall not be a natural ability, but the gift of God. For it is one thing to be God, another thing to be a partaker of God. God by nature cannot sin, but the partaker of God receives this inability from God.

There shall be accomplished the words of the Psalm, "Be still, and know that I am God." (Ps. 46, 10) There shall we be still and know that He is God; that He is that which we ourselves aspired to be when we fell away from Him, and listened to the voice of the seducer, "Ye shall be as gods," (Gen. 3, 5) and so abandoned God, who would have made us as gods, not by deserting Him, but by participating in Him.

This Sabbath, if we count the ages of the world as days, will be found to be the seventh day. The first age, or the first day, extends from Adam to the deluge; the second from the deluge to Abraham, equalling the first, not in length of time, but in the number of generations, there being ten in each. From Abraham to the advent of Christ there are, as the evangelist Matthew calculates, three periods, in each of which are fourteen generations—one period from Abraham to David, a second from David to the captivity, a third from the captivity to the birth of Christ in the flesh. There are thus five ages in all. The sixth is now passing and cannot be measured by any number of generations, as it has been said, "It is not for you to know the times, which the Father hath put in His own power." (Acts 1, 7) After this period God shall rest as on the seventh day, when He shall give us rest in Himself. There we shall rest and see, see and love, love and praise. This is what shall be in the end without end. For what other end do we propose to ourselves than to attain to the kingdom of which there is no end?

I think I have now, by God's help, discharged my obligation in writing this large work. Let those who think I have said too little, or those who think I have said too much, forgive me; and let those who think I have said just enough give thanks, not to me, but rather join me in giving thanks to God. Amen. (30)